MW00932091

DIVORCE
SUCKS.
NOW WHAT?

*The 5 Steps to Find Yourself and Heal After
Going From "I Do" to "I'm Divorced"*

WENDY STERLING

Dedication

For my mama.
You will forever be a muse of inspiration to me. While your time on this earth has passed, you are with me every day in my heart. Thank you for being my trusted guide, my best friend, and my source of inspiration. I love you always.

Introduction

I will never forget the day I knew my 15-year marriage was over. My husband and I were driving home after having an amazing dinner in Beverly Hills with another couple. We listened to music and cruised up one of the canyons to get home when his phone rang. It was 11:45 pm. He quickly declined the call, trying to make sure I didn't see the name pop up on the screen of his car. Except I did, and suddenly I felt a punch in my gut. Was it my intuition or was it paranoia? Either way, I knew something did not feel right. Why was she calling him this late?

I knew the consequence of making an accusation first discovered by my intuition, but I didn't care. The last time I did that, I was gaslighted and made to feel crazy and delusional. I was tired of silencing myself and feeling trapped in my own mind, throat, and body. And as I dusted off the voice and identity I had long desired, I became stronger by the minute. The universe was telling me to speak up. It was my moment to be heard and that I was not crazy. While I was terrified of what my words would mean for my life (and my kids' life), I knew nothing could be worse than the Facebook façade life I had lived the last few years. You know, the one where you post smiling vacation pictures on social media when, in reality, you constantly fight behind closed doors.

My pulse was quick, and my stomach was in knots as I uttered the words I dreaded saying out loud. "Are you having an affair with her?" Even while my heart was breaking, I felt a weight from my chest lighten. So that is what using your voice to express your truth feels like? It didn't matter if he heard me. It was about using my voice to express my feelings, thoughts, and truth. That night, everything changed. Her phone call woke me up and gave me ownership over my life. I realized I had the power within me to stop the cycle I had perpetuated my whole life—looking to others to show me who I was, what was possible, and how I felt.

In this book, I will share how you, too, can use divorce as an empowering experience to find your true identity and voice to create the life you want instead of feeling stuck with the life your ex left you with. As someone on the other side of an unexpected divorce, I am here to tell you that there are silver linings. While I know you may not be able to see them right now, by the end of the book, you will know you and your spouse are better apart than together. It starts with being open to the idea that your divorce is happening FOR you, and it will require some work from you. It will also require you to take 100% responsibility for your life and how you got here. Marriage takes two people. So does divorce. Are you open to seeing how this will free you and allow you to soar on the other side? It's time for you to release the pain of the past and fear of the future, so you can live in the NOW—the only true time that exists. When we stay stuck in the past, we tend to focus on the half-empty glass and make excuses for what they or we did wrong. That is precisely what is stopping you from moving through the pain. Yes, divorce SUCKS. No, you did not plan on your life looking like this and neither did I. However, since my divorce, my life has been WAY better than I could have ever imagined.

When we spend time in our heads thinking about the past, the lack in our life, or pointing fingers at others, we are creating a lonely, sad life for ourselves. After all, you create what you think. You have more control over your thoughts than you allow yourself. Instead of thinking about what your ex is doing or who he is with, use that time and energy to think about the life you want to live. Do you want to feel happy, peaceful, free, and confident? It is all possible. You still get to live, even though your marriage died. And no, your divorce does not have to be finalized for you to start living. It starts with your mindset. If you choose to put your life on hold while waiting for your divorce to be over, you will miss what happens in your life along the way. The journey is a big part of this healing process. Take advantage of the beauty around you, the learning, the clarity, the connection, and the love. It just takes shifting from seeing life through a glass that's half empty to seeing it half full. Consider your divorce a wake-up call with no snooze button. The faster you wake up, the quicker you will get on with your life. You will be okay, I promise. Just put one foot on the floor at a time. It is the same regardless of age, even when you are single later in life. You get to choose to live NOW.

Here I am on the other side, telling you what is possible, and you are at the start of your process wondering what you will make for breakfast or if you will wake up tomorrow without crying. Or perhaps you are on the other side, still angry, bitter, and seeking closure. You may be on the hamster wheel of life where you feel stuck, triggered, stressed out, overwhelmed, afraid of the unknown, freaking out about your financial security, and full of doubt—to name a few. I know the list is long, and they are all valid feelings. And to top it all off, you don't feel seen or heard - not when you were married and certainly not in your divorce. It didn't matter what you did or didn't do. Nothing you tried worked. You feel taken advantage of, abused, neglected, and forgotten. I was there, too. I picked fights to feel seen and most certainly heard. I would text him a lot to remind him I existed and get mad at him for not acknowledging all I did for him and the kids, all while dying inside. I was a people pleaser seeking people's attention, recognition, and love, especially in my marriage.

Sound familiar? Even if only one thing I said sounds familiar, you want to keep reading. You are like me in some way. I know you have probably done some things already, like Google searches, joined Facebook groups, listened to podcasts, read books, watched free webinars, or searched for "Fear of the Unknown After Divorce" YouTube videos. You've done some work, and yet you are frustrated because it isn't working or isn't working all the time. You get mad at yourself when you don't apply the learning, or you fall back into autopilot because it is easier and more natural. The thought of a new life is more terrifying than staying in your old one. You know you want out, yet you are afraid of what that means and looks like. Or perhaps you didn't ask for a divorce, yet here you are. Maybe you've grown apart and still think you can try to fix it. After all, that is what you do. You fix people and things. But do you? Does fixing people work? Does controlling others with your words or actions work? I am guessing the answer is no. And yet you keep doing it thinking the "next time," it will work. Or one more text and "they will get it." And they don't.

We do everything in our power to resist healing and change because we don't know what is on the other side. This book is intended to show you what is possible if you take the steps you've been resisting for far too long. It will take work and discomfort, you will have to rewrite your internal narrative, and you may lose some friends along the way. After all, you are modifying your identity and sense of self through your everyday life. Divorce is a process that requires you to get outside of your comfort zone and eliminate the need to feel liked by everyone. I can promise you that what is meant for you on the other side of your divorce is everything that is meant to be in your new life. Much like the process of metamorphosis when a caterpillar spins itself into a cocoon and emerges as a butterfly. Your divorce is a time for you to reinvent yourself. While butterflies don't need help transforming, humans do. Butterflies trust that the cocoon will break when their transformation is complete. Humans have a hard time surrendering and releasing control because we fear the unknown on the other side. Because every divorce is different, we don't have certainty the same way as a butterfly.

What if I told you there is a way to feel that certainty? I will share those ways with you through some hard truths throughout this book—and I do so because no one else in your life will be honest with you in the way I will. I am not here to hurt you or make you feel bad in any way. I am here to tell you what you don't want to hear (and know you need to) because what you are currently hearing is keeping you from moving on. It is keeping you from the peace, freedom, happiness, confidence, and ease you so desperately desire. Our friends and family care. I know mine did and they also kept me stuck. "He will regret this" or "you will wake up in two years and see how this was a blessing" were phrases I heard all the time, and they did not make me feel good. I could not wrap my mind around those thoughts because they felt too far away. Our friends and family try to take us out of where we are - the pain - because they don't want to be there with us. And that is exactly where we must stay to get through this more quickly. I invite you into the cocoon of divorce with me. Yes, that is where the shortcut to recovery lives—staying in it and feeling through every emotion and pain point to get to the other side more quickly.

That is where I come in. I stay in the pain with you until it feels lighter and you're ready to fly like a butterfly! We don't stay there for long because we don't have to. I go in with you, holding your hand and cheering you on as you push through it. And then we come out on the other side, still holding hands, and you feel relief and a bit tired. Why tired? Because you have been carrying around the weight of those emotions for TOO long, and they were really heavy!

When we carry our emotions around, they become an albatross to our ability to move forward. No wonder it is hard to build a life you choose when you are trying to build a new one using rocks that don't fit anymore. They are not going to serve as the strongest foundation for your new life. It is going to take leaving those rocks behind and learning what new foundation your life gets to be built from. If you keep trying to use the rocks you have been carrying around, it will take a lot longer to build. I know those rocks are familiar, and you've been keeping them "in case." However, I invite you to toss them starting today. They are not coming with you as you build your new life. They can't. It will take unlearning old patterns and behaviors, learning new skills, developing new practices, and a willingness to heal your past traumas. It will take work, and it takes less work when you have the right tools to get through it. The tools I give you in this book will help you heal inside and feel the outside world shift as a result. You will get your voice back, so you will feel heard. We will remove the invisibility cloak you've been wearing to reveal ALL of you. The tools will show you how to love yourself and build your confidence, self-esteem, and worth back stronger than ever before! Now is the time to create your new foundation on your terms, without permission, and from your heart.

This book will give you the steps to build a new foundation for your life. However, it is not a pre-made, cookie-cutter foundation. It's not for someone who wants to stand around reminiscing about the old rocks. It is not for someone who throws the rocks at her ex, claiming to be "giving them back." It is also not for someone who is unwilling to take responsibility. This book is for those who are tired of carrying the rocks around because they know they are not serving them and are seeking a way to put them down with grace, compassion, and love. That is how you will heal more quickly and who this book will truly serve.

Given my own experience, I lend my expertise to those who have been through similar experiences and emotions as me. While I was mentally manipulated and lied to, I was not physically abused, nor were my children. I understand that people who are in or have experienced domestic abuse may be drawn to this book. However, it is not designed to serve you. I speak and coach from the lens of experience, education, and authenticity, so it is just not in my wheelhouse. I am not trained to support spousal abuse on either side. Therefore, this book serves those willing to work through their emotional divorce trauma to see their divorce as a gift—an experience that is happening for them. This perspective does not let your ex off the hook or have anything to do with them. This is about you. I want *you* to want this for yourself more than I want it for you. I want you to stop letting your divorce define you into shame and to see it as empowering the way I did.

You will be okay, I promise. Even when you are single later in life. Are you ready to live the life you desire now? Keep reading.

Chapter 1

I still remember the sickening moment my life changed forever. As I sat there next to him on the drive home from our couple's night out, I kept thinking to myself how it didn't make sense that she was calling him, especially so late at night. Sure, they were colleagues, but was that really all she was to him? The voice inside of me wanted to scream, "What the fuck?" but I couldn't get the words out of my mouth. I was paralyzed with fear as my mind started racing, and my heart began to pump out of my chest. I knew they were work friends yet being around her always made me really uncomfortable. Anytime I brought it up to him, he told me I was wrong and saw something that was not there. They were just friends, nothing more. Except now I knew I wasn't crazy to believe something more was going on between them. It was more than a crush on either side. She was calling "her person" that late at night, as any of us would if we needed to vent and find comfort. This time the gut punch I felt was hard and intensely painful, which I recognized as a sign that my worst fear about them was coming true.

I looked over at my husband and, after a moment of silence, asked him why she was calling him so late and why wasn't he picking up the phone. He stared at me blankly and dismissed me, saying she probably got into a fight with her boyfriend and he would call her back when we got home. I pondered his answer and then asked, "Then why is she calling you and not her BFF Carrie?" He had a comeback for this question as well. He replied that because he is friends with them both (her and her boyfriend), he is good at helping them mediate and diffuse their arguments. I thought about it, and while it sounded reasonable, it also felt like a manipulative lie. Sure, it made sense on the surface, and yet my gut was unsettled and told me it was wrong. I stared out the window and felt my mind racing with millions of questions. *Did she always call when they were fighting? How often did they speak? What was really going on? Did she want my husband? What the hell was going on between them?*

I was so scared and confused and didn't know what to think or do. I never had a reason not to trust my husband for 20+ years until now. Suddenly, all of what we built and created was dangling off a cliff, ready to break into millions of pieces.

I sat there in the car next to him, stewing in my panic and fear, which then turned into anger. My head was flooded with voices telling me versions of what was going on. *They are just friends. They are way more than friends. Stop being so paranoid. She wants him. He would never cheat.* Nonetheless, I knew deep in my gut that a line had been crossed between my husband and his coworker. It became so clear at that moment, and I wondered when I stopped paying attention to the distance between us. My mind started to race again as I questioned whether all the fights and disagreements we had over the years pushed him into her arms. It was not in his character to do that. However, I was so doubtful. I was confident in his love for me and our boys and I could not imagine he would ever do this to us. The more I thought about the possibility of her and my husband together, the larger the rage inside me grew. However, it wasn't just rage, it was a voice that felt familiar. It felt trusting, calm, and supportive. And then it hit me—it was my voice. The one that was silenced when I was a little girl.

As a young child, I had a lot to say and many opinions, most of which were not popular. After years of being told I was wrong, dismissed, and told to stop talking, I lost the will to use my power and voice to express what I was feeling and thinking. I was afraid to speak up because that meant I might ruffle feathers or stir the pot, so to speak. It was ingrained in me, so I naturally silenced myself and allowed my voice to become one and the same as my husband's when I got married. Anytime I had a feeling inside my body where something felt off, I talked myself out of it due to fear of consequence or abandonment. The few times I tried to speak up, I was told I was wrong—by my family and my husband.

For the remainder of our drive home, I kept myself silent, turned my face away from him to stare out the window at the night sky, and began to cry. Tears streamed down my face as the reality of what was really going on hit me. This was more than just a friendship. When I turned my head to the left to look at my husband, I could see fear in his eyes and yet could not figure out if it was because he got caught or because he wanted to help his friend. Regardless, his speed increased, and the silence was deafening as we pulled into the driveway of our home.

When we got home, I marched straight back to our bedroom, and he followed shortly after. I asked to see his phone, and he said no because he was going to call her and see what was going on. He walked out of our bedroom and called her from the other side of our home so I would not hear him. He was gone so long that I finally went to bed with no resolution and a large wedge between us. We never went to bed angry until that night. I left the house the next morning to go work out without saying goodbye to my husband. I don't think I've ever worked out so hard and with so much adrenaline before. The faster I ran, the clearer my mind got as I replayed the night before over and over in my mind. Each version of the phone call confirmed what I believed to be true, and the only way I was going to get answers was to see his phone.

The moment I got home, I asked our boys to go upstairs because their dad and I needed to talk. I could see the panic in my husband's eyes and knew I could not back down. This was happening! There was no going back now! It was time for me to muster up the courage and strength to take a stand for myself. I spoke one sentence, "I don't like how her call made me feel, and I know something more is going on between you two." Immediately he started telling me how she got into a fight with her boyfriend, and he had to help calm them both down. I didn't buy it. I refuted and said, "It's weird that she calls you, and I don't like it. I want to see your messages with her. Give me your phone." Without missing a beat, he said no and that was all I needed to hear to confirm what I knew was the truth. At that moment, I decided it was time for him to leave our home. I needed to calm down, and he needed to go somewhere else.

Being in his presence made me sick to my stomach. I didn't want to be around him, nor did I want to see him. I looked him dead in the eyes and said, "Get the fuck out of my house, NOW!" He looked at me in disbelief and proceeded to tell me how irrational I was being and how I was blowing this call way out of proportion. Of course, it was my fault. How could it be his?! I was not going to waiver from what my gut was telling me. There was something not kosher about the two of them. It did not feel right, and I was not getting the answers to tell me otherwise. He was deflecting and not being direct. I told him to pack a bag and leave immediately, or I would throw his clothes on the lawn for all of our neighbors to see. The choice was his. He went to our bedroom and, 10 minutes later, walked out the front door with a small bag in hand.

After the door shut, I collapsed to the floor shaking, crying loudly, and screaming, "What is happening?" I could hear the footsteps of my seven and ten-year-old boys coming down the stairs, and I tried to breathe and calm myself down. They stood above me, looked at me, and asked why I kicked their dad out of the house. I told them I felt disrespected by their dad and that we needed some space from one another. Kicking him out of the house was painful because I knew my boys heard me, and at the same time, it was the first time in my adult life that I used my voice and stood in my power. Immediately my boys blamed me for breaking apart and ruining our family and said they would never forgive me. My heart was broken already, and that just dug the knife even deeper. I allowed the knife to stay there for over eight months. I bore their pain and blame, and my ex never said anything to the contrary.

I didn't know just how hard it was for my husband to be honest and tell the truth until that night in the car. He and I were in couples therapy for two years before to help us learn how to better communicate with one another and did not know how to let the other feel seen or heard. We both had childhoods where communication was a struggle with our families. Neither of us learned how to use our voice, so we brought that dynamic into our marriage. I thought the way to be heard was to raise my voice or pick fights, which did not work. I had no other way of knowing what else to do, so I took our therapist's advice each week and really worked on making our communication and marriage stronger. What the hell was he doing for all those years?

I poured my energy into my marriage, husband, and career and lost my sense of self along the way. I was so focused on everything and everyone else that I didn't know any other way. I was on autopilot, going through the motions of my life without being conscious of my actions until now. I was fully aware of what was going on, and it was both terrifying and liberating. I had no idea what I was doing and felt more out of control than ever before. So, when I woke up the day after I kicked my husband out of the house, I realized that it was a school day, and I was alone. Getting my kids out the door that morning was a challenge, but I managed to do it with a fake smile on my face.

When I got home, I went into our bedroom and noticed my husband's iPad sitting on his nightstand. I felt a rush of energy that pushed me toward his side of the bed to grab it and open it up. I heard a voice say, "Open it, read it," so I started to search his email for her name, and I remember saying to myself, please be wrong over and over in my head. Of course, I was not. A flood of messages appeared with pictures, love letters, daily check-ins, flower orders (sent the same day I received flowers), and so much more. In shock, I threw his iPad so hard at the wall I dented it and fell to the floor, crying and hyperventilating. My first panic attack. My hands were shaking, and my breath staggered as I called my best friend and told her what I had discovered. She begged me to stay where I was and not do anything because she was on her way over.

When she walked in the door, I handed her the iPad, and her jaw dropped as she read the same emails I just went through. After knowing him for 20 years, she could not believe her eyes either. I needed confirmation from her that I was awake, that this was not a nightmare. She helped me see I was not crazy. My husband and I had couples therapy that night, so she helped me come up with a strategy to confront him in the safety of our therapist's office and stressed the importance of me not calling or talking to him before. We were driving separately to the appointment, and it was crucial for me to give him a chance to be honest with me. She was optimistic that he would be honest with our therapist in the office, so she helped me calm down and see that there was hope. We got the emails ready to show as the worst-case scenario, and she assured me that everything was going to get resolved that night.

I'd never felt so nervous before in all my life as I made my way to our couple's therapist's office. It was the longest 25-minute drive of my life. I had his iPad in my purse, with the most damaging of emails on the screen. He was late and walked into our therapist's office after me. After he sat down on the couch next to me, I immediately confronted him about her call the two nights before and their relationship. He chuckled and instantly denied that something was going on and told me I was reading into things. I then slowly reached down into my purse and pulled out his iPad, and his face went ghostly white. Ha, I got him! I turned it on and said, "Then what the hell is this?" His jaw dropped, and he was speechless for the first time and said nothing. To me, that was his admission of guilt. I started crying and hyperventilating, which then turned into a severe panic attack where I thought I was having a heart attack. I couldn't catch my breath, and he just sat there staring blankly at me. He didn't show concern for what was happening, nor did he try to help me calm down. No words, no actions, nothing. I was devasted. Not only did he lie to my face when he was confronted with the truth, but he also couldn't even fall on his sword. Seeing my physical reaction didn't faze him, and he broke my heart into even more pieces. I've never felt more alone, sad, and depleted in my life. It became crystal clear to me that the last two years of couples therapy had been a complete waste of time. The effort I had put into us and myself felt embarrassing—even stupid. And so was investing in our marriage and the future I thought we both were working towards.

We decided it would be best to separate, and over the next year, we stayed in couples therapy and individual therapy. He told me he was committed to working on our marriage at any cost, so I clung to that hope with all my strength. While I was learning about how my childhood dynamic played out in my current marriage and life, I also found myself continually stuck in the past. I kept going back to what he did, what he didn't do, what moments over the last 15+ years of our marriage were real, what was not, how he had the time to have an affair, how he could do this to our kids, and the list goes on and on. I was drowning in the memories and stories of our past. Nonetheless, I kept searching for answers thinking it would appear the harder I looked. In fact, I looked so hard that I prided myself on being a really great private investigator. Any new piece of evidence I gathered, the stronger I thought I was becoming when in reality, it was tearing me apart inside. My life as I knew it was over, and I could not grasp the reality of that. I felt like I was living someone else's life. That was the only explanation I could give to help me get through this. I convinced myself that there was going to be a piece of evidence to show me this was not as bad as I thought. After all, I was a strong and independent woman and would fix it. I would fix him, change him, make him choose me. I believed I could handle the emotional roller coaster all by myself. I thought one more book to read, one more podcast to listen to, one more free online class, and I will be one step closer to the answer to get me unstuck and to figure this out. I had hope, yet there was a lot of doubt behind that hope because nothing I did worked. I kept wondering, why isn't this working? After eight months of therapy, reading self-help books, and listening to podcasts, why was I still feeling so doubtful?

During that time, I saw a Facebook post from a friend who became a life coach helping women discover their next chapter. At that moment, I wondered what life coaching was and recognized that voice as divine intervention, which came in the form of a physical gut punch, telling me to reach out to her—NOW! So, I did. After speaking with her on the phone for over three hours, I immediately realized that focusing on my future was what was missing from my healing process, and that was the focus of life coaching. It gets you focused on the now, to get present to what's happening today, and to envision where you want to be in six months, one year, etc., and create the steps to get there. It was time to try life coaching, so I hired a coach and decided to enroll in learning how to be a coach. I thought if I did both, I would move through the pain even more quickly. Since I am a go big or go home kind of gal, that was my mentality and what I felt the universe was telling me to do. So, I listened.

It quickly occurred to me that I spent years, decades really, living my life looking in the rearview mirror, constantly wondering, "What if?" I always used words like "should," "ought to," or "I really need to do that one day." Those statements leave room to make excuses, back out, put others first, and not honor your word. I always came up with excuses, pushed timelines, and put other people first, especially my kids. It was never the "right time." However, in order to feel like I was moving forward in my healing and figuring out if I wanted to stay married, I needed something I clearly wasn't able to give to myself, which was accountability. And that fact was hard for me to admit. I am a Type-A personality, a control lover, and a people pleaser. After trying to fix me and my marriage alone for so long and still feeling stuck, I had to admit to myself that I needed help. I had to try something new because I was doing it alone for too long and not achieving the results I desired. So, I signed up for the course and hired a coach—after all, isn't that what credit cards are for?! Working with a coach is an investment— more so than working with a therapist. While I had no idea where the money was going to come from, I knew that in time I would figure it out, and it would be worth it!

Best. Decision. Ever. What I learned blew my mind! In fact, in just two days of learning what coaching is, being coached, and coaching others, I had moved through more of the emotions around my husband's affair than I had the entire eight months prior in therapy alone! No joke! It blew my mind. I wondered where this had been all my life and why wasn't anyone doing this work for divorced women. At that moment, I knew there was something special about this work, and my divorce was not happening to me but for me. That had to be the answer because why else would this be happening in my life? It chose me. I was going to bring this work to the world and change lives. I knew I was not the only one who had to be feeling the way I did. I didn't ask anyone because I was so ashamed and afraid they would see me as weak and powerless. And yet, at that moment, I saw the incredible power my separation had given to me. The more I learned and received coaching, the faster my healing process happened. I was able to relate the tools to my experience in a way I had never heard before.

Those closest to me started to see a shift in me. Well, everyone except my husband. I was learning who I was, what I wanted, what I was not willing to tolerate, how to set boundaries, what loving myself felt like, and ultimately what

I wanted my life to be from this moment forward. It was time to take control of the wheel of my life and decide where I was headed. So, my husband and I agreed to meet in our couples therapy office to discuss whether we were going to work on our marriage or part ways. It was almost one year to the day I discovered his affair, and I felt it was time for us to make a decision. Thinking back to that day, I was ready to say let's work on this. My mentality was to see if our marriage was salvageable based on where I was, who I was learning I was, and who he had become. From where I stood, I could see that he was becoming more hands-on as a father when he had custody of our kids. I also felt how appreciative he was for all I did when we were married because he realized how much work it takes to raise two boys. He led me to believe he was learning a lot about himself and what he wanted, which I assumed was to stay married. I was so confident that he would LOVE this new version of me and had no doubt in my mind he was going to say let's work through this.

The silence between us as we sat in our therapist's office was deafening. My stomach was in knots, my head was spinning, and I was breathing shallowly. The space between us felt like miles, even though it was only two feet. When our therapist asked how we wanted to proceed, I let him go first. He proceeded to explain how he was still confused and unsure of what he wanted. I was shocked. *WHAT?! Can't you see how amazing I am and what you are going to lose? Look at me. Look at the work I have done, don't throw me/us away.* Frustrated, furious, and exasperated, I looked at him and had an out-of-body experience. The words that came out of my mouth were not mine. I heard myself say, "Well, I am tired of waiting, and I've made my decision. I want a divorce."

I suddenly came back into my body and thought, wait, what?! What did I just say? What just happened? Not wanting to look stupid and to stay in my power, I looked at our therapist and asked if I could leave. She replied, "Yes, of course," and I walked out the door. I didn't stop until I got to my car, and streams of tears ran down my cheeks. My breath was quick, and I felt a panic attack coming on. I quickly opened my car door and slid into the seat, putting my head on the steering wheel as I said aloud, "What did I just do?" Over and over and over again. I peered at my reflection in the rearview mirror, trying to make sense of the last five minutes. I was unclear about what I said, yet more sure of my decision than any other one I have ever made in my life.

Then why did I feel so scared and alone. Shaking, I started my car and called my best friend. She immediately picked up and asked me what had happened. I told her through my tears and choked-up voice that he still didn't know what he wanted, so I ripped off the Band-aid and ended our marriage. She listened as I cried, realizing I was single for the first time in my adult life. Single with two boys. Two boys who had no idea what I had just decided and how their entire future would forever change. Two boys who meant the world to me. I would have stayed to avoid putting them through any more pain. But I knew that I couldn't be with someone who didn't want me and who I didn't trust. Asking for a divorce was the first time I chose to stand in my power and choose myself.

Little did I know the ripple effect that choice would have on the people in my life. My decision sent a wave of energy through the universe that would change not only my life and my boys' life, but my mom's as well.

Chapter 2

The day I told my husband I wanted a divorce was also the same day that I received a call from my dad telling me my mom was rushed to the ER, and they found ovarian cancer. Still in shock from the morning's events, I was numb and in disbelief as I hung up the phone. My heart sank, and my stomach churned. How was this happening to me? To my mom? Not now, not today, not ever. I cannot lose my mom, too. My mom and I were closer than close. She was my best friend, my go-to shoulder to cry on, my biggest fan, and my rock. Yet on that day, September 5, 2017, she was diagnosed with Stage 3-C ovarian cancer, and I was confronted with the news that she was dying. I was devastated two times over in one day. The two people I thought I could count on forever were both leaving my world, even if on different timelines. My mom and my husband were my foundations, my rugs, my everything, my people. The ones I counted on to be there forever, no matter what. In the course of a few hours, they were no longer "for sure," and I was suddenly faced with the prospect that I would lose them both.

My mom had always been a fighter, an optimist, and one of the strongest women I knew. Yet I knew this cancer battle was going to be her biggest challenge to date. And here I was, alongside her, fighting my own battle as well. My mind was consumed with thoughts of "why is this happening to me?" I could not understand why G-d would take away my mom when I needed her to be healthy now more than ever. I remember flying home to San Francisco from Los Angeles on what felt like the longest Southwest flight of my life. The plane could not fly fast enough, nor could my Uber driver drive fast enough to the hospital. I ran to her bedside upon arrival and remembered seeing her lying there with tubes and machines around her. I walked into her room and walked up to her to kiss her gently on the forehead. She woke up and saw the sorrow, fear, and sadness in my eyes and immediately started to cry. Hours before, I had called to tell her what happened in the therapist's office, and now here I was with her as though the morning's events had taken place weeks prior. She was apologizing between sobs because she didn't want to die and leave me when my marriage was coming to an end, and I was crying because I was grieving the loss of my husband and the knowledge that I was losing her, too.

I was determined to give my mom a reason to fight. Reminding her that I asked for a divorce brought a smile to her face, and she said, "Good for you. You deserve so much better. You deserve the world. Dad and I are here for you no matter what." At that moment, I knew I gave her the will to live, to fight the cancer, and to support me as I transitioned from a life as a couple to being single in my 40s. We would fight alongside her by doing research around alternate treatments, diets, and energy healing to see what more we could do besides get her into the best ovarian cancer medical trials. Research and distraction were the perfect combinations to avoid feeling my divorce wounds because I didn't want anything to take me away from whatever time I had left with my mom. Not even my career or my divorce.

It was during my mom's first year of chemotherapy that I witnessed just how invasive her treatments were. Watching her lose her hair, lose sensation in her fingers and toes and not be able to stomach food for days was painful. I knew this was going to be a long road for her. However, I wasn't aware of the emotional impact it would have on me. Living 350 miles away made my sorrow that much greater. I felt helpless and couldn't just sit back and watch her go through this. I felt in my soul that there had to be alternative ways to help my mom cope with the effects of the chemo and slow down the cancer. My mom was open to anything and everything that would prolong her life, so she was open to ideas and suggestions outside of what her doctors were recommending. I was well connected in the coaching world and knew someone had to have a suggestion for me.

When you ask the universe for support, it delivers and oftentimes brings people into our lives for a reason. The new mastermind coaching group I joined happened to have a few different types of energy healers in it. I connected with and met a woman in the group who talked about her business that helped her clients using ThetaHealing®. Theta-who? Theta-what? She shared how it has lasting effects on trauma wounds and frees you from the negative energy that feels like a dark cloud. It is a meditative technique that works with the Creator of All That Is (aka the universe, G-d, etc.) to help you clear limiting beliefs and live life with positive thoughts. In other words, it brings harmony to your mind, body, and spirit. I know it sounds "out there," and I was open to *anything* to help my mom. Little did I know it would help us both.

I always like to try doing work on myself before doing work on others, so I decided to work with the ThetaHealer® I met and scheduled a private 1:1 day with her. I wanted to not only learn more about the process, but I also wanted to see how the technique could help me shift my beliefs around my pain and grief about my divorce. So much of my grief was tied to this deep-rooted feeling that my ex-husband and I were in a past life together and soul mates. I felt like I knew him better than he knew himself. Our souls were connected in a way that I could physically feel a burning sensation and throbbing on my chest when we would be communicating. I felt his energy on a scar on the upper left side of my chest. It was where I had a melanoma removed, and the scar is a straight line, about two inches long, and is located just above my heart. My heartbreak felt literal, and eventually, I came to see it as the place where he broke my heart. Just touching it felt painful, like a lingering, dull pain that stung and didn't go away. At random times, it would throb with pain, telling me my ex was up to something that would reveal itself in time. The scar was a spot where the spiritual cord that tied us together was yanked out, but part of it was still wedged inside of me. It enabled me to still feel connected to him and all that he was doing (wrong). I called him my soulmate for decades and felt connected to him on a deeper, soulful level as though we had been in multiple past lives together. I could feel his presence around me and lingered like a dark cloud. His energy stole my light or, worse, lived off of my light like a parasite. I was his light, love, everything, and it depleted me. Every interaction with him was painful and exhausting. It was like I was being sucked back in, only to be stabbed in the heart all over again.

During our 2-day ThetaHealing® intensive, I experienced something like never before. My healer used crystals to support the belief work, so she placed a clear crystal on my heart while we meditated and invited in Creator of All That Is to help with the healing of my wounds. She completed a soul fragment retrieval between us energetically—I gave him his energetic fragments back, and he returned mine (no, he did not have to be present for this to happen). Think of soul fragments as pieces of energy that are embedded into you. The fragments were cleansed and healed prior to returning them to one another, and I could feel the disconnect as it was happening. Within seconds, after he and I disconnected energetically, I felt a spark ignite on my scar, and I jumped backward. My eyes sprang open, and I looked at my healer. Her eyes were open and staring right back at me. We both knew at that moment that something powerful had happened—my heart restarted. What I mean by that is my heart's beat restarted using a new rhythm. A rhythm that was all mine without him. I felt a calm rush over my body, and a release of tension flowed through my fingertips.

I'd never experienced anything so powerful and long-lasting as ThetaHealing®. The day my heart restarted, my heartbreak ended. It was the strangest yet coolest experience. When I would think about him, what he did, and who he was with, I could not feel him or his energy. I literally felt nothing. Not the nothing where you are numb. The nothing like you don't give a shit. I felt free! The pain was gone like it never existed, and it was instantaneous and long-lasting. To this day, it has not come back. I don't feel him the way I used to. Sometimes I try to feel if it is still there, and it isn't. The cord was officially cut forever, or at least in this life.

Cutting my bond with him also allowed me to explore the beliefs and feelings I had from my childhood and how they manifested in my marriage. When I look back at my life, I see that it was shaped by a long line of very strong women in my family. Their bravery, strong opinions, and the very loud voices were used to create better lives for themselves. These women taught me that my education was important, along with marrying a doctor or lawyer. Oh, and he should be Jewish, or I was disowned. Bye, bye. The language spoken was, "Do as I say, and you will go far. Do as you want, and you will no longer be a part of this family." So, I learned at a very young age to silence my voice and let my elders speak for me even when I disagreed. The one time I spoke up and expressed a different opinion than my grandmother, I was immediately silenced and told I was disrespectful and wrong. So, I always did what was expected of me, as most little girls do. Looking back, I realized that I was living life through someone else's eyes and using someone else's words. I learned that if I used my own, I was in danger of disrupting the status quo and, even worse—I would be abandoned by the very people I loved the most. The danger in this lesson was that it became my normal, and I brought that behavior into my marriage. I allowed it to happen.

Nothing else I had done up until that point worked like this. I also knew there was an order to how my healing would benefit me, and I was doing it all at the right time. Before this, I was not ready. I was not spiritually open to this kind of healing. It took baby steps to get here. And I learned how to be patient with the process. It was part of my teaching to my mom. To be patient and trust in the universe, Creator, and G-d that they know our path. To allow Divine to lead. When my mom heard about my ThetaHealing® experience, she was pleasantly surprised. And we both knew the power of ThetaHealing® would help my mom. If I could heal my broken heart, I would find a way to heal my mom's cancer. Nothing was going to stand in my way, and my mom knew it. I could feel in my soul that there was something about this work that would help her. The goal was to prolong her life alongside the chemo and to try everything. She was open and gave me her permission to give it a try on her! Without a second thought, I enrolled to get certified as an Advanced ThetaHealer® so I could take the Diseases and Disorders class and immediately start doing energy work with my mom.

That voice inside of me that said to do this for my mom was what I have come to recognize as my intuition. Don't get me wrong, I used to hear that intuitive voice inside me as a young girl, and over the years, it got quieter and quieter. I was so used to being muzzled I forgot how to summon the strength to rip it off. It wasn't until I discovered my ex-husband's infidelity that I finally found the courage and willpower to end the cycle of silence. After all, how could I be silent from that moment forward? Look where staying quiet got me—divorced. My voice was worthy of being heard, and I had nothing to lose. I could speak my truth instead of what made everyone else happy or my ex look good. I learned not to worry about what other people would think. I found the courage to speak and learned how to communicate from my heart as WENDY for the first time in my life. And to me, that was priceless.

You cannot put a price tag on your worth, yet as a mom, we do. We analyze anything and everything that might help us, yet when it comes to everyone else, we don't give it a second thought. Looking back, I would have spent any amount of money to move through the healing process if I knew it would work. And when it comes to medical treatment, I want the best of the best for my loved ones. No questions were asked about the cost. Yet when we think about something that could help us, we consider whether we can "afford" it. Many times, we say we cannot and go as far as to say "not now" to imply "later" is an option. We all know it is not. It is our way of making ourselves feel better for putting ourselves last (if not second). Yet if you knew your child needed a very specialized procedure, would you delay the procedure, or would you find the BEST surgeon in town who is available ASAP? If your schedule was packed, would you clear it out without hesitation? The latter for both, right? So, what is the difference between you and your child?

I can tell you the difference— it's how you view your worth and value. Like me, you do not regard yourself in the same manner you do others. Why? When did that start? Or has that always been how you've operated? In my marriage, I had no trouble spending on my kids or husband. I never questioned the baseball gear or the movie tickets or dinners out. However, when it came to me, I thought about it and thought about it and thought about it some more and always said no to myself. I thought of all the things I could buy for my family and found it selfish to think about me. Thinking about me meant taking away from others. My ex-husband reinforced this message—as the breadwinner, he could do as he liked even when I worked full time. He spent our money, and I became resentful because it was never on me. I expected him to read my mind and buy me gifts, treat me to spa days, and tell me to take a Sunday morning to myself. He took care of himself, and I expected him to do the same for me. During our divorce, I realized he was taking care of someone else – it just wasn't me. Suddenly I was faced with the reality that it was up to me to think about myself and to use my voice when I needed something. My divorce gave me the green light to start thinking about myself. To think *for* myself and to do it starting now.

What I learned watching my mom fight cancer is that the only time that truly exists is the *now*. Not the past and the future hasn't even happened yet. So how could I use my time to envision the life I wanted regardless of time, money, or circumstances? Sure, hiring a coach was a great first step, and I started to see results when I invested in myself. Working with an energy healer cleared a major block in my heartbreak that nothing else cured as quickly. All of this was so far outside of my comfort zone of asking for help. I needed to stop making excuses about money and time and fill the gap of what was missing in my healing process. That key was someone helping me envision the life I wanted and to tell me what I was doing wrong along with what I was doing right. I knew help was going to come with a cost and learned that cost was an investment in me.

When I pre-paid a trainer and set an appointment to show up at the gym, my ass got out of bed because I paid for him. And if I didn't show up, I lost money. Hiring a personal trainer is not cheap! The money I paid him is what made me accountable. There was nothing to keep me from doing the hard work at the gym, especially when I was paying a lot of money for the body I wanted to have. Similarly, I worked hard for my income, and to just throw it away because I am lazy was not an option. The game changer for me was accountability. When you don't hold yourself accountable, you feel guilty, make excuses, push appointments off, and/or get discouraged. A lack of accountability also means you do not fully own everything that happens in your life. You do not take responsibility for your attitude, your actions, your reactions, your communication, and your relationships. Instead, you blame others or try to fix things. If you want a different outcome, take ownership, like getting your ass out of bed when you tell yourself you will. Otherwise, there will be consequences. Consequences are actions, and they come at a cost.

There is a difference between costs and investments. There is a return on your investment, while you do not get anything back or long-term gains on a cost. So often, we attach a cost to our worth instead of seeing our worth as something we invest in. Divorce is not cheap because it is worth every penny. Let me remind you of something—so are you!

Think about how much time you have spent listening to podcasts, reading books, and attending free courses. How many months, how many years? I have clients who waited years before raising their hands and asking for help. They watched and followed me, listened to my podcasts, joined my free Facebook Group, The Divorce Rehab, and stayed at arm's length. The consequence they paid was sitting in suffering longer than they wanted to because their ego's voice saying, "You can do this yourself," got in the way. Living with anxiety, resentment, bitterness, anger, guilt, and shame, all to prove they could do it alone. Yet, the people who pay the biggest price, aside from yourself, are your kids.

So here comes the tough love I am known for because I will always tell you the truth. The only person responsible for where you are now is you. Not your ex. What I know for certain is that when you get out of your own way, silence your negative voices, and remove your victim and fear mindset, life gets so much easier. We think the opposite will happen, which is why we like to stand in our own way. I started feeling better instantly once I pushed through the resistance, fear, and discomfort of asking for help. Asking for help was really, really hard for me. Why? I thought it would make me appear weak. What I quickly learned is that you are stronger when you use your voice and ask for what you need instead of pretending. I didn't understand the concept of using my voice in a constructive way to feel heard until my 40s because of my upbringing.

What I've learned is knowing who you are and your worth is more important than anything in this world. Your bank account does not measure your worth. You are worthy of anything and everything this world has to offer. You are worth investing in, no matter what. Investing in you means using your voice to command the life you desire, and sometimes that means hiring people who know better than you how to solve your problems. I wanted the proven roadmap to get me there faster. I wanted the right team in place to get me there quickly. That meant spending money on experts with proven track records to ensure my future and my kids' future would be secure. It is a marathon, not a sprint. Invest in your future self and life rather than letting your fear of money or lack thereof today keep you stuck or in an unhealthy marriage. It is worth every penny!

Chapter 3

Yes, divorce is expensive. If you are like me, it ends up being more expensive than we anticipated at first. Way more expensive. Sure, you pay your lawyers' fees (along with that awful, expensive retainer), you find yourself seeing your therapist even more, and perhaps hire a financial advisor that specializes in divorce along with a divorce coach. In my case, the list of bills got longer the deeper I dug into my husband's affair. Suddenly, I am paying a forensic accountant, hiring a CDFA (Certified Divorce Financial Advisor), and a new accountant. As I was gathering the paperwork together, I realized that so much was mysteriously missing, and bank account amounts were low. I was already freaked out starting over on one income, but I thought I had more of a nest egg to rely on until we were knee-deep in our divorce process.

Suddenly, the reality of our financial situation smacked me upside the head. Overwhelm and fear took over. When did I stop paying attention to how much money we had and what we spent it on? How did this get by me? For the first decade of our marriage, I was the one who managed our money. However, when I had our second son, I experienced postpartum depression and needed to release more responsibility to my husband. My OBGYN referred me to a therapist who I started to see, and we worked on me not taking on everything in our house. The one area I agreed to relinquish control over was our finances, and my husband willingly took it over. Instead of still staying close to the numbers and knowing our bills, I turned a blind eye for sanity's sake and trusted he would handle it. In retrospect, it was a huge mistake. However, at the time, it was what was best for me, given my mental state.

Here I was faced with the fact that our bank accounts were low, and our credit cards had debt piled up on them. Not once in my life had we not been able to pay off a bill. That was how I was taught to live and what I budgeted for in our marriage. I had to take responsibility for handing it over with little to no guidance and trusting he would figure it out. With this new information staring me in the face, I wondered if it would just be cheaper to stay married. I got so scared of what I was going to be responsible for, and I was so ashamed of myself. How did I not know this was going on? I worked my ass off making money in a career I hated. I traveled, entertained clients at night, and left for work early every morning. For what?! It quickly dawned on me why he wouldn't agree to let me quit or start my own business. He needed my income to afford his double life.

I went back and forth in my mind about staying married to avoid the financial mess we were about to find. In my gut, I knew that this was not a reason to stay or take him back (if he would consider it). Thoughts and images flooded my mind. When did he have time to cheat? Would I ever be able to trust him again? Would I ever see a dime of the money back? I then wondered who else he had cheated on me with. Were there other women? What else was I going to uncover? The more questions I had, the more I wanted to dig and uncover the truth. The more facts I found showed me the sunken depth of nefarious activities he got himself into. What if other people found out about this? What would they say? What would they think of me? What would happen to my kids? How would they be treated differently? Would they be shunned the way I was feeling? Would I lose more friends? What would his family say and think about their golden child?

The fear of "what ifs" flooded my mind and created more confusion and doubt. Was pulling the trigger on the divorce worth what the embarrassment and knowledge were going to cost me? Is staying with him better because together we can accumulate the money back faster? What if my parents found out about this? They would be so ashamed of me, so angry, so disappointed. I couldn't stand the thought. It took me weeks to tell them about our separation – how was I going to tell them money was missing? After all, I was the first person in our family to get a divorce. I was already feeling shame and embarrassment. And then it occurred to me that maybe when he discovered I knew what he did, he would want me back. Or the thought of his parents finding out would force him to take me back because they are the last people he would want to disappoint.

When my attorney informed his attorney about our findings and desire to hire a forensic accountant, my husband wrote me a letter that was delivered to my attorney that I have still not read to this day. I have no plans on ever reading it. Instead, my attorney summed it up for me as she knew it was going to make things worse. In the letter, he admitted to being blackmailed and a long list of justifications for why he had to play along. My first reaction was, "What an asshole. Get some balls!" My next gut response was, "Wait, if he admitted to being blackmailed, that means there is A LOT more to uncover. Hire the forensic accountant to know for sure." Whatever money it would cost, it would be worth it in the long run. Peace of mind is priceless. Since we had to go down this route, I was going to make him pay either way.

Money was flying out the door during every stage of our divorce, and while there were moments I was terrified about paying all these bills, I also knew that it would cost me more if I did not do my due diligence to get the facts I so badly wanted. I had to keep my head on the long game and think about my ability to care for my kids down the road. He was never going to tell me everything or the truth, so I knew that I had to use the evidence to piece it together. I remember approaching my husband multiple times and begging him to tell me the truth so we wouldn't waste money on all these fees (after all, it was college tuition money going out the door). He claimed he told me everything, and in my gut, I knew he was lying. Anything to make him look good and save face.

It was an eye-opening moment for me. He was choosing himself and at no point chose our kids or even me. Why was I giving him the power to choose for us? The only person who has the power to choose me is me. As I learned from my life coach, taking my power back meant choosing me 24/7. I was in charge of my own peace of mind and sanity. I had control over my emotions and the facts I found. And other people's opinions are none of my business. My parents and friends shared their opinions with me, and while I sometimes agreed, there were times I did not because they were not living my life. They were also not inside of my body listening to my intuition. Trusting my internal voice and standing in my power were two huge steps I learned and mastered going through this process.

That internal voice is something we people pleasers lose connection with over time. We think we are being selfless because it would be considered selfish to do as you want. What about our spouse? Was it fair to them? It reminds me of my client Rebecca who came to me unsure of whether she wanted to get a divorce or work things out with her husband. She felt so lost and unsure of herself and her choices. Her husband was manipulative and used his health as a yo-yo to bring her back. We worked together to get crystal clear on who she was outside of being his primary caregiver and the breadwinner. Who was she after years of marriage? Was she still in love with him vs. loved him? While her desire to start a family was a reason to stay, she also didn't want to tie herself for life to someone she may not want to stay married to. She went back and forth about it daily, and at each turn, I reminded her not to get ahead of herself. There was healing to do and new behaviors to learn.

Slowly, she was starting to see how over the years, she changed and became what he needed her to be for him to thrive. By separating and moving out, she was able to discover not only life without him but who she was, what she wanted, and why she wasn't going back to her old life. Together we worked on her self-confidence to communicate her feelings (her husband was a narcissist, so it takes a specific way to speak to feel heard) and explained what she needed from him to make this work. He claimed he was doing the work, and after six months, she saw that he wasn't who she desired in a partner and the father of her future child. She chose divorce.

My other client, Debbie, had an affair and was unsure if she wanted to work on her marriage the way her husband did. She was terrified about the financial implication and the impact a divorce would have on her kids. She was overwhelmed with fear, unhappiness, and a lack of self-worth. She didn't feel appreciated or seen in her marriage, and that was why she strayed. She justified it by saying her husband was "not that guy" who was overly expressive with emotion. And during our sessions, we uncovered her inability to clearly communicate her needs to her husband. She operated with the belief that he could read her mind and see what was missing. She was not alone.

Many of us make the mistake of thinking our spouses are mind readers. I know I did! When we do this, we take away our own voice and power and instead leave it in the hands of another. Together Debbie and I worked on what she knew she deserved in her marriage. It took her separating from him, moving out, buying a new home, and living life apart to see that she wanted to work on their marriage. They decided to reconcile. Doing the work on yourself means figuring out what works best for you. It isn't about moving forward with divorce. It is about moving forward with the choice that is best for who you have become and the future you want to create.

Unlike Debbie, I wanted a divorce. To be clean, clear, and free from the manipulation, deceit, and lies he created and could not walk away from. After being given multiple chances to be honest, he chose to tell lie after lie after lie. Lies that cost us a ton of money. How could I be with someone who would rather lie than tell me the truth? I knew my truth and chose based on what I knew was best for my boys and me. Continuing with the divorce was the best choice for me because, with each step, I reclaimed and found another octave in my voice that I had lost decades before. Pulling the trigger meant choosing me vs. waiting for him to want and choose me.

Accountability starts with you. It is up to you to model the behaviors that you want to embody to see a change in your life. You are accountable for all your successes and failures. Taking accountability is not a one-time thing; it's an always-time thing. When you are held accountable by someone else along the way, you are supported anytime life goes awry. You are given praise and encouragement along the way, which is incredibly motivating. When we are not held accountable by others or holding ourselves accountable, we feel discouraged because we are shifting the blame and giving our power away. We find ourselves retreating and not standing in the power of our voice. We also focus on what we are not doing instead of what we are doing. We point the finger outwardly and say our circumstances are someone else's fault. Accountability is about stepping into your power of voice and inspiring confidence in yourself.

Accountability is the accelerator in divorce recovery. When we choose to be accountable, we are willing to take an honest look at how we have contributed to or co-created the situations and circumstances in our life. We release the blame we put on others and instead stand in our power of voice over how we've co-created our life. Our focus shifts to owning how the way we have chosen to show up created the life we had. Accountability keeps you focused by taking ownership of how you acted, spoke, and showed up in your marriage. If you don't own your side of the street, you will continue to repeat the same behaviors. You need somebody to challenge you and call you out on your shit, while encouraging you to push through the hard stuff, the mess, and the ick.

Chapter 4

Saying and sticking with my decision to move forward with our divorce brought up many fears and conflicting emotions. One moment it felt freeing, and then the next, it felt terrifying, overwhelming, and exhausting. The process was an adrenaline and anxiety-filled roller coaster without the seat belt. The kind where you question WTF at every bump and turn. Yet anytime I decided or made a choice about my future, I felt a physical reaction in my body that forced me to pay attention to what it meant because it either paralyzed or energized me. I quickly learned the physical reactions I was feeling were more of an internal compass guiding me back to my self-confidence, trust, and self-respect. It connected my mind to my heart and my soul, and my intuition, all of which were linked to what I learned are my core values. Values are a part of who we are and who we want to become. They help guide us to prioritize what is important to us as they provide direction, help us feel more grounded and make better decisions, and with them we are overall happier. Ultimately, they are the foundation for your life and your marriage.

My divorce taught me how values can make or, in my case, break a marriage. When we started dating in college, life felt easy. We would meet up between classes, have a date night on the weekend, study together, and go to the movies. Being together was fun and easy! We saw the world in the same way at the age of 18 and we knew there was the potential for a future together. After all, he was smart, came from a good Jewish family, wanted to become a lawyer, would make a great dad, etc. He checked all the boxes on paper. However, we slowly grew apart after having kids, and our relationship changed. When I looked at my values, I realized our values did not align, nor were they prioritized in the same order. It made me wonder how much of my value system I saw in him when we got married. I was so caught up in the excitement of having a diamond ring on my finger and getting married that I let the endorphins take over. I saw us as soulmates, destined to be together forever. He was my person. My best friend. The universe brought him to me because he checked all my boxes. But did he check my values boxes? Therein lies the reason we got divorced.

Values are qualities or characteristics that we bring into our actions every day; they help us become who we are most proud to be. They are often referred to as our personal guiding principles or life goals that are not specific to any one situation. Knowing your values is like having a life compass that guides you in the direction you want to live your life, get your bearings, and adjust as needed. Values are not the same as goals in that there is no endpoint. It is about the journey of honoring your values along the way. These values may evolve and even change, but there will never be a time when you check a value off your list as "completed." Therefore, it is important to align yourself with and get clear on what is truly important to you. Values guide our behavior in every single point and place in our life—home, work, social life, and parenting, to name a few. At the end of the day, values guide our beliefs, our attitudes, and our behaviors. My top values include honesty, respect, connection, and love. Given that my husband cheated and lied to me about it, his values were not in alignment with mine, and I wondered if they ever were.

People change, especially so during life transitions like getting married, having a baby, and getting a divorce. At times they are one version of themselves, and in others, you hardly recognize them. Things that were important decades ago are no longer important, or vice versa. People change, as do their values. When values shift, they shift not only you but your relationship. When we are around those who do not share our values, we eliminate joy from our lives, and we feel it in our bodies and know it in our minds. The same holds true when we do not know our values. we run on the hamster wheel of life, which inflicts suffering and dissonance in our lives. For me, it's that uncomfortable feeling I get in the pit of my stomach or a gut punch or a twitch when I know something doesn't feel right. Think about the last time you said "yes" when you wanted to say "no." Do you remember the inner conflict you had? Where did you feel it? What did it feel like? That is the signal when you know a value is not being honored. Brené Brown says in her book, *Dare to Lead*, "Our values should be so crystallized in our minds, so infallible, so precise and clear and unassailable that they don't feel like a choice – they are simply a definition of who we are in our lives. In those hard moments, we know that we are going to pick what is right, right now, over what is easy."

Do you know what your values are and why they are important to know? Identifying your values and taking committed action towards them, even when it is uncomfortable or difficult, is how we gift ourselves with living a life of vitality, meaning, and true fulfillment. Having clarity around our values is important because it allows us to make decisions in alignment with who we are and what our truth is.

There are three benefits of identifying your values:

1. Values assist you in situations where you have the choice to react or respond.

   Values are guiding principles for our behavior to ensure we show up as the most authentic version of ourselves. I often reacted quickly in difficult situations due to a "charge" of energy I felt in my body. I didn't always take the time to breathe, pause, and think about what I was doing or saying before I did it. I just jumped, hurdled, or threw a fastball instinctively. Checking in with your values gives you that time to "take a minute" and choose to respond in a thoughtful, respectful manner.

   My client, Valerie, used to get triggered every time she received a text message from her ex-husband. Her mind would race, her blood pressure would increase, and her response was more of a gut reaction attack. We've all been there, haven't we?! When she learned how to pause and take four deep breaths in and out, it immediately slowed her heart rate, and she found herself in a calmer state. She realized that most of his messages did not require an immediate reply, so she started giving herself two+ hours before responding. It took willpower to not write back immediately, and she quickly learned how she was able to stay true to who she was when she wrote him back.

2. Values reconnect you with your authentic self.

Many of us lose our identity in our marriages and don't realize it until we are faced with divorce and living as a single adult. That was my experience along with all of my clients, and it feels more like a whack upside the head with a two-by-four telling us so. We have no idea who stares back at us when we look in the mirror. Instead, we see a shell of someone we used to know, someone who got lost along the way, and we desperately want to find them again. Because we've been on autopilot for so long, we've forgotten what we think, want, like, or feel. So many of us just went along with our spouses' ideas and decisions because it was easier. I know I did! Or perhaps we adopted our parents' beliefs because that was expected of us, or we learned to stop using our voices. We wanted to avoid confrontation or the fear of not being liked.

My client, Christina, cared deeply about what other people thought, and so she lived life paranoid and sought approval from others. She was always in a serious mood and had a regimented daily schedule because that was how she was able to keep herself going. And yet she was miserable. We did a values exercise together to discover that one of her core values of fun was not being honored in her everyday life. It was a jolt to her system that inspired her to take action. She was committed to making a change, so she started having dance parties in her kitchen, volunteering more at her kids' schools, and making plans with friends when her kids were with their dad. Her kids even commented on how different and fun she was! The power she felt in just making small changes in her daily routine and staying flexible helped connect her with herself and her kids.

3. Values increase your confidence and happiness.

When you learn what your values are and learn how to honor them, it brings a sense of calm, confidence, and safety to your life. In those moments when you feel that discomfort in your body or punch to your gut, it is a value being questioned. Thinking of which one it is helps you to know what decisions align best with that value, not what is best for the other person or for you! It reminds me of my client, Linda, who had a value of connection that her ex-husband tried to push against on a weekly basis. She valued her weekends with her son, and her ex conveniently purchased sporting event tickets on her weekends, seeking custody for an outing with their son. She said yes every time because she was so afraid of disappointing her son, and yet she was the one who felt the disappointment because she treasured her weekends with him. We worked on what language she could use to set boundaries with him around her values, and she committed to saying "no" the next time he asked. It happened just a few weeks later, and she was so surprised. She called me and said she could not believe how well her answer we prepped worked. She said he simply replied with "okay," and that was the end of it! She was firm, respectful, and clear. When you are clear in your own mind about what you want and what is important to you, it becomes less important what matters to other people. This assurance naturally brings a sense of confidence to your life. It is a step-by-step process, a marathon, not a sprint.

The more you recognize your values as part of your internal being, the easier you will make choices based on those core values. A simple way to identify a value right now is to think about something that angers or annoys you. Perhaps it is dishonesty. The opposite of that word is your value— honesty. Discovering your values is easier than you think! It is those words that you feel in the core of your being that are pieces of you. For me, my top two values are integrity and respect. What are yours?

So, you're probably wondering how you apply your values to the recovery and healing process of your divorce. It becomes the foundation you go back to every step of your journey. Your lawyer calls with information from your ex's attorney, or your ex-spouse text you, and you get annoyed. You pause and reflect on what value is being dishonored based on the information you are given or what you are experiencing. For me, it was a constant poking at my value of integrity. So, I got to align with my value in my response to my attorney rather than allow my emotions to set off a wildfire. Knowing your value(s) helps you understand why you feel triggered and reactive and helps you calm down to respond without emotion.

While a lot of emotion is involved in a divorce, at the end of the day, it is a business transaction. Bringing in our roller coaster of emotions makes the process much harder, longer, more complicated, and more expensive. In fact, it forces you to play the short game vs. the long game. Slowing down and understanding what is happening inside of you and knowing what you have control over will give you back your power and voice. It will also show you quite obviously why you and your ex are no longer compatible. Knowing my values was another tool to reinforce why the choice to divorce was best for my children and me. My ex and I did not align in any of our values. Or perhaps the fairer way to rephrase that is we choose to honor our values differently, which makes us incompatible. It's amazing what happens when you honor yourself instead of honoring what is important to your spouse!

Not honoring your values creates and stores negative energy in your body, home, and in your external interactions. It makes being around you miserable and painful because you have an aura of misery. Ultimately, it is not healthy for you, your kids, or your home. Your values are your compass, your North Star. They are what you go back to when you are questioning something or feeling triggered. When you fight against your values or don't check back in with them, you choose to default back into a people pleaser, where you find someone to complain to after the fact. My guess is that you don't want to do that anymore, correct?

The way to end the people-pleasing game and use your values in your decision-making process is to put boundaries in place. For example, if your value of respect is not being honored, you may end a conversation with someone. Or if your value of honesty is being tested, you may end a friendship or be guarded in what you share with that person. Values help us to know what boundaries in our life we get to create or learn how to stand in our power to enforce them. Boundaries are rules, limitations, and guidelines you create to help others know how to interact with you. They are meant to help strengthen the relationships in your life while providing you with the self-respect and self-love you know you deserve. Many times, we have a hard time enforcing them due to the inner dialogue in our head that typically comes from our inner critic or ego judging us. Those voices create fear and guilt in our minds that prevent us from standing in the power of our voice and values. This is the #1 reason my clients have such a hard time living in alignment with their values and enforcing their boundaries! They think that the inner voice projecting fear is theirs when it actually isn't! In the next chapter, I will dive into how to distinguish between your inner voice of fear and your true self to get unstuck, release your pain and suffering, and start on your path to healing and recovery. To learn more about how to set boundaries, you can get more information about The B Word boundary course in the back of the book.

Chapter 5

I am always asked what the magic pill is to end the pain, anger, and sadness or when a person will start to feel better. Isn't that what we all want—to move away from the discomfort and just be done? Unfortunately, what I have to say is not what you want to hear because there is no magic pill! If there were, I would have invented it by now because nothing was going to stop me from moving out of my pain! I thought the magic pill would be found inside a book or while listening to a podcast. So, the more I consumed, the more I believed I was getting one step closer to getting rid of my pain. And I kept making the same mistakes—I thought there was one thing that would heal me, and it would happen immediately if and when I found that one tool! Boy, was I wrong! It took me a lot more time and money to figure it out, so I am going to pay it forward with my wisdom in this book.

Want to know the shortcut to feel better? It is to feel through the pain, ending the thoughts around the emotions and surrendering to the flow of emotion no matter what it looks or feels like. Yes, that means it will get worse before it gets better. In order to be free of your ex and your divorce emotions, you need to heal the root causes of your suffering. The closer you get to those root causes, the more pain you'll encounter.

The reason we put a stop to feeling the pain and emotion from our divorce is because it does not feel good, and we judge ourselves or fear others will if we don't stop. It doesn't matter how long you have felt this way, it is just what happens, and we all do it! We think the voice in our head is us, and I am here to tell you it is not. While we all struggle with negative voices and self-talk, we have a hard time stopping it because it sounds so believable. We also believe it is our own voice. You may even notice a voice inside your head constantly evaluating why these changes could never happen—you're not capable, everything you do is wrong, you'll regret it, or a variety of other distorted thoughts that sound quite believable! And that voice has our best interest in mind, don't they?

Let's talk about why and when that inner voice starts speaking. Close your eyes and think about a time in your life when you wanted to make a change, try something new, or ask for help. Then as you mustered enough courage to take a step towards those changes or experiences, what emotions first came up for you? Did you feel anxious, nervous, or fearful? When I think about my answer to that question, which was asking for a divorce, I was all three simultaneously! So, you are not alone! I could not help but hear all those warnings inside my head telling me everything that could go wrong! We all have a self-criticizing voice or voices, and quite often, they are more like self-sabotaging voices that hold us back and shift our perspective to the glass half empty. You know the voice I am referring to. It's that voice in your head that says, "Why bother trying? It's not going to work," or, "You can't do it, so don't try!" or, "You can't do this. You will fail." These inner critic voices inside your head can:

1. Store all the rules on how you "should be" or what you "should do" and then threaten to punish you if you don't follow them.

2. Bring to the surface all of the negative stuff said about you growing up (family, teachers, friends, coaches, etc.), and remind you of it constantly!

3. Stop you from trying something new even if you make mistakes along the way. Many times, you give up or don't try. However, if you do try something new, you are on high alert every step of the way to avoid

making a mistake because you're afraid of the consequences.

4. Continually criticize and compare you to others to determine success or failure.

5. Store the voices of parents, coaches, and teachers (people you want to please) who project their expectations of you and impact your choices, decisions, and behavior to avoid potential disapproval.

Let's be real - listening to your inner critic is depressing. When your inner critic runs the show, your relationships, work, life, and self-esteem plummet to the ground. It feels like you can never do anything right, no matter how hard you try. That is why you constantly feel crappy, anxious, and burnt out. It is exhausting to listen to. Now here's the catch...would you believe me if I told you that your inner critic wants you to be happy? I know, please hear me out...

According to Hal and Sidra Stone in *Embracing Your Inner Critic*, your inner critic is formed in childhood to protect you. "[Your inner critic] developed to protect your vulnerability by helping you to adapt to the world around you and to meet its requirements, whatever they might be. It makes you acceptable to others by criticizing and correcting your behavior before other people could criticize or reject you. In this way, it reasoned, it could earn love and protection for you as well as save you much shame and hurt." The requirements that make you acceptable to others can come from your parents, caregivers, teachers, religious leaders, friends, media, society, and past hurts. So, if your family taught you that it's inappropriate to show your emotions, your inner critic will criticize you when you do so. If your teacher used to put you down, your inner critic will push you to work harder. On a bigger scale, our society promotes a certain image of success that your inner critic constantly compares you with. Your inner critic might demand that you look impeccable at all times, not be too emotional, needy, loud, opinionated, or selfish, must never ask for help to avoid appearing weak, work hard with little or no play, and the list goes on and on. What we do know is that we live in an uncertain world. We have little to no control over outside circumstances and people, which scares your inner critic because they want to ensure you feel loved and accepted. So, your inner critic attempts to control you by molding you into the world's criteria and expectations.

While your inner critic has good intentions, it tends to go on a power trip. Your inner critic wants to minimize your pain above all else—even if that means avoiding the necessary risk it takes to change for the better. Worse, many people unconsciously identify themselves with their inner critic's voice, which further disempowers them: You're stupid → I'm stupid. If you can't tell when it's your inner critic's voice, you are more likely to believe its mean remarks. When you don't live up to your inner critic's unrealistic standards, you feel inadequate, unlovable, and flawed at your core. Our inner critic strives for their version of perfection. The thing is, no one lives up to their inner critic's standards because they aren't realistic. When you reject any aspect of your personality—the good or the bad—you're harming yourself. We're all human. We have "defaults" and make mistakes. To feel happy and fulfilled, we get to stop judging ourselves and embrace who we are. Flaws and all! As kids, we didn't know better. Many of us did not hear, "You're good enough" or "You're beautiful as you are." However, it's never too late— you can learn how to accept yourself now so that you have a choice in how you show up in the world.

When you distinguish yourself from your inner critic, you can live life on your own terms. So, believe it or not, you're not broken or flawed. In fact, without breaks and gaps within you, how can you grow? You have believed your inner critic for too long. It's your turn to lead and end the negative beliefs and talk. Shifting your perspective will impact who you become today. In order to be your best self tomorrow, it will require you to step out of the dark (aka the fear) and, instead, step into the light (aka self-love).

Want to know how? The first step to do that is to pay attention to the message underneath and ask yourself, what is my inner critic guiding me towards? For example, if you hear your inner critic say, "You stupid idiot! Why did you have to say that? Now nobody will like you," reframe the message to hear what is really being said, which is "I'm scared nobody will like me because I said something I felt was silly." Do you see how what is underneath the message is a fear of not being liked? So, the reframe becomes easier to engage with because your rational brain is empathizing with your fears. This is why I said your inner critic is trying to keep you safe, even if it isn't going about it the right way. It's okay for your inner critic to take a break or be gentler. You're listening, and you won't allow it to be cruel. What is important in this step is to recognize the important point it is trying to make, just not in the kindest of ways.

To shift into kindness requires gratitude. No matter how hard you try to gracefully navigate the tough times, your ability to express and receive gratitude for whatever is going right probably feels like it's waning by the second. Practicing giving and receiving gratitude requires placing intentional focus on the positive, which I know can be difficult. We default to thinking the worst and hoping for the best. We believe that when we prepare for the worst outcome, we will be prepared no matter what. What we prepare for is the outcome we don't want, and it makes having gratitude that much more difficult. However, gratitude can be hard, especially when your mind takes you down the pity party and victim road. I chose that road partly because I wanted others to see the impact of what his cheating did to our family and me. I thought it would give people a reason to call me and give me an excuse to call others. Let's be honest, it is an easier default and party invitation to give out. There is comradery in pain. It is a tie that binds people together.

In fact, it was one of the many bonds that my mom and I shared. We were having a "why me" pity party at the same time. It was an invitation given out to those who we knew would attend and join in on the fun. The *fun* others brought to my party looked like telling me all the reasons why my spouse was a loser, how he will regret his choices, why I am better off without him, how life is not fair, and so on. My mom's pity party fun sounded like, "You will be okay, and you will beat this. Cancer sucks, you have so much to fight for, and you have so much to live for." Those are the *last* things you want to hear when you are in the thick of misery and pain. In fact, you are not really thinking about any of that. You are just trying to wrap your mind around that moment or the next hour of your drastically different life. I was terrified of my new life alone and being labeled as a divorcée. My mom's fear was dying.

In fact, we would talk on the phone about it all the time. She would keep me stuck in the story of what he did by saying, "I would have never thought he could do this," or, "I still can't believe he cheated on you, what an idiot! Doesn't he know how lucky he is?" It would further my anger, frustration, sadness, and betrayal. In turn, I would tell my mom, "This is so unfair!" or "Why is this happening to you?" We dug one giant pity party hole with each negative statement we spoke out loud. Not once did we try to find a silver lining in it. Instead, we kept ourselves in the quicksand pointing outside to find the person responsible. For me, it was my husband. For my mom, it was her doctors.

Of course, it feels safer to point the finger outside and seek answers externally. And the more people you can share with, the more chances you have to get people on your side. When people are on your side, it justifies your finger-pointing. However, what ends up happening is that it is all you talk about, and over time, no one wants to be around you as much. In fact, you push people away. No one wants to hang around someone who constantly complains, cries, and gets angry when you bring up the same topic—your divorce, your ex, or your cancer. Over time, your friends don't know what to say anymore because after all this time, you are still talking about it, and nothing they've said seems to help. While they pull away, so do you.

There is a lot of shame and embarrassment that comes along with divorce, and instead of feeling the pain of it all, we turn it into a bitch-fest. We seek others to join and tell us how we feel is correct. Hence the pity party. I remember it was the topic of my life whenever anyone asked me how I was. I would tell anyone that would listen how my husband made the biggest mistake of his life, how he was going to regret this, and what he was doing with his life that was wrong. My "what's appropriate" filter became non-existent. I didn't care. Slowly, friends disappeared and stopped inviting me out. I was left with my oldest best friend, and she was the only one I could turn to on my bad days (which were daily). I told her I was afraid she was going to abandon me like everyone else, and she assured me she wouldn't. And she didn't, no matter how many times I called her crying and venting. Unfortunately, the constant storytelling I was telling myself about what he was doing or how I was feeling because of him did not lessen. It was getting worse the more I kept thinking about it.

There is a difference between thinking about it and feeling through the emotions around it. I slowly realized that instead of moving through my feelings and thoughts, I was diverting the responsibility to my ex. It was my responsibility to feel through the pain no matter what because I was a co-creator of it. What I mean by that is that my pain was a result of the role I played in my marriage. Instead of walking around saying I was angry, I went deeper into why I was angry and blamed him. I wasn't acknowledging my role in what happened between us at all. On the surface, my pain was rooted in his cheating. However, when I went deeper inside me, it was because he did not pick me. I did not feel chosen. BOOM! There it was—the emotion I avoided by staying in the anger. He did not choose me.

When we stay on the surface with our emotions, we perpetuate the victim mindset and pity party. No one wants to be a part of that. And it prevents us from taking action. You think you are in action talking about your anger. However, the action involves digging under the surface and healing the true wound - feeling not chosen or, in other words, unseen. Whenever I spoke up as a child, I stood out because I didn't always say what others agreed with. So instead of feeling encouraged to stand behind my beliefs and opinions, I was told I was wrong and to be quiet because I was drawing attention to myself. I chose a "louder" man than me, and I relied on him as my voice. After decades of being silenced, I used my voice to ask for a divorce. Realizing the sound and power of my voice was a huge game changer for me and my healing because uncovering the true wound is when real healing can begin! While part of that wound was tied to feeling seen and heard, ultimately, it was about being picked. My divorce gave me the power and voice to pick ME.

Chapter 6

Hearing the sound of your voice for the first time evokes emotions you don't anticipate. It also uncovers pain you've been avoiding because you are uncertain of where it will take you. Allowing yourself to go deeper into the pain you are feeling helps to clear the surface fog so you can see your true path to healing. Everything you've been through is rising in your consciousness, and it is your job to see yourself through and out of it. Going deeper means we have to go more than just surface level, and it is going to feel uncomfortable. And when I say surface level, what I mean is beyond just the mind work. I was in therapy and working with a life coach, and yet I still felt stuck and tied to his every move. That is why it was important for me to do the ThetaHealing® work in myself that I talked about earlier.

Because of its immediate and long-lasting impact, I knew of so many others who would benefit from this type of healing work. The results I saw for myself when I used therapy alongside coaching and ThetaHealing® accelerated my healing. Don't get me wrong—I am a huge fan of therapy. However, I do not believe it will completely heal you alone. Therapy was great at helping me see how my childhood shaped who I was today. It did not solve the deeper soul and energy connection I felt. The piece that needed to be cut was not something you could see, per se. So, I decided to get certified as a ThetaHealer® to help my clients on the body and soul side of healing. I knew I was not the only one who needed this or would benefit from it, and it was a game-changer for me.

My ThetaHealer® teacher not only helped me shift the beliefs that were passed down to me from my family, like "to stay safe, you had to be silenced" and "money is a weapon to use against people," but she also freed me from my ex-husband's energy hold over me. It was the disconnect from him that I needed to see that being alone and single versus alone and married in my forties was a blessing and the best decision for me. It meant peace and freedom. Having a clean slate to start over and create the life I wanted to have felt doable. I was no longer looking at his life and comparing myself to him because I loved myself. Suddenly I did not feel so alone being alone.

There is a difference between being alone and feeling lonely. These are two different states, and only one negatively affects one's well-being. It is possible to feel lonely even when we are around other people. That may well be how you felt in your failed marriage. That is how I felt. There is a difference between being alone and married and being alone and single. The former feels worse than the latter. ThetaHealing® allowed me to release my ex-husband, see how his energy was holding me back, and trust that I would be okay without him. As a result, it allowed me to stay open to being a co-parent and start dating because I no longer felt a connection to him. Many of us think about staying simply because we fear that no one will ever love us again. We rationalize the thought by thinking we are not getting any younger. We have the responsibility of raising our children. We are too wrinkled for a good-looking person to pay any attention to us, etc. We believe there is truth to our words. Let me be the first to tell you they are not true in many ways. People date at all ages and in any shape or financial state. Perhaps you fear that you will turn into an old cat lady or die alone. These fears are not directly linked to your idea of love or of relationships, they come from your pain of the past and fear of an uncertain future.

I had been with my husband since we were 18 years old, and the thought of online dating was terrifying. When he and I met back in 1998, dating apps weren't a thing. We met in college through friends at a fraternity party. Fast forward to 2017, when I was single and surrounded by nothing but married friends. How in the hell are you supposed to meet anyone when everyone you know is married? Is dating in your 40's the same as dating when you are younger? HELL TO THE NO! I was mortified because I had no idea how to date or meet someone online without the fear of being murdered on my first date. In fact, I set up a text thread with my best friends so that anytime I went out on a date, someone knew who I was with and where I was, and I would check in mid-date. I was overloaded with so many fears whenever I thought about dating. Where do you start? How do you start? I learned from first-hand experience that you have to just rip off the band-aid! It hurts at first and then becomes no big deal. I didn't know that at the time, as I am sure you have experienced or will. And when you dip your toe into the dating pool, you start thinking, "Why do I have to do this again? How did I get here? What will someone see in me that is appealing? What makes me special? Who will want me?"

Someone did, and his name is Jeff. I kissed a lot of frogs to find my prince. And it was worth every second. With each date, I learned more about myself and how to communicate and interact with men. I learned how to use my voice and to listen to my intuition. Red flags were usually gut punches that told me, "Date is over," or to ask more questions to confirm the flag should be flying. It was a great way for me to build my dating muscle and get confident along the way. Over five years, I dated my fair share of men, some amazing and others not so much so. A part of me needed to get it out of my system, and then it got old. While I had one long-term relationship before Jeff, I never felt like he was the one. It made me question if I was ever going to find a partner, a best friend, or someone to spend the rest of my life with. I wanted to know when I was going to find him—would I ever find him? Would he find me? Where is he? Why haven't I met him yet? How many more guys do I have to date to find him?

This line of questioning myself mirrored a lot of what my mom was experiencing. We were both stuck in the dialogue loop around fearing the unknown. My mom was questioning her mortality and G-d. She asked questions like, "Why me? Why did I get cancer? Why me when I am a good person? How do you live knowing you are going to die? How do you fight to live when you know you are going to die?" My mom and I spent nights on the phone crying while sharing our fears with one another. We kept asking why us, and yet it made complete sense why it was us. We were going through this together, and for a reason. The universe was conspiring again. It sure didn't feel good or like something either of us wanted. However, there was a higher purpose at play. My mom was suffering, I was suffering, and we leaned on one another to lift the other. I looked at what she was going through and thought to myself—Wendy, you have your life, you will live. Meanwhile, my mom looked at me and thought to herself that she would fight and live because her daughter needed her. In the end, neither one of us was going through this alone. It felt lonely on some days, sure. On all the other days, we had one another and an amazing support system of people who had our best interests in mind.

My mom was one of the reasons I decided to get certified as a ThetaHealer®. I had done some research and spoke with some other ThetaHealers® to learn that this modality of energy healing had been used with diseases. I am a firm believer that the mind is a powerful healing weapon, and I thought it would be another "thing" to try in healing my mom. Given her diagnosis, it was one more avenue to explore, and she literally had nothing to lose. It was never meant to replace her medical treatments. It was intended to see what it could do alongside it. There was so much to gain. Regardless, it would give me the opportunity to support my mom and help keep her mindset positive. After all, your mind can be your greatest weapon, or you can let it be your nemesis. It's important to train your mind so your body is at its peak performance.

What we think creates the future we will have. Our thoughts inform our actions and our words. What you believe in is ultimately what you receive and create. If you think that you are useless and unlovable, it is a natural consequence that no one will love you simply because you do not allow it to happen. The challenge with managing your old belief system on your own is that your consciousness will hide your inner truth from you. Think about it—when you accuse yourself of something, your mind starts to rationalize and give you valid reasons for doing things the way you did. Humans are naturally resistant to change. If you acknowledge that something is wrong with you, your consciousness sees this as an impetus to change, and it does everything possible to avoid the message. However, if you notice that you are having negative thoughts about yourself, it means that you have something to heal within you before moving into a new relationship. You cannot think badly of yourself and expect to find the love of your life. It's just not going to happen. It's natural to long for the kind of connection you once had early in your marriage, but your priority now is to find, rediscover, and love all of you from the lens of your own eyes, not someone else.

I felt deeply connected to my husband and called him my soulmate. He knew me, and I knew him. I loved him, and he loved me. What he loved about me, I loved about me. What I loved about me was based on his opinion, his reflection, his everything. Without him, without my mirror, what was there to love? For a long time, I saw nothing. I saw a middle-aged single mom who was depressed, anxious, angry, bitter, and starving herself—who would want me? My eyes were swollen, and I walked around like Eeyore. What was there to love about what was left now that I was single with kids? Being married meant security in knowing someone loved me and saw what was lovable about me. Being divorced meant I was unlovable and undesirable. In the end, he didn't choose me. However, for the first time in my adult life, I chose myself when I asked for a divorce.

When we don't love ourselves, flaws and all, we are blind to what makes us amazing. We spend so much time thinking about what is wrong with us or lacking within us that we stay disconnected from our truth, our soul, and our authentic self. Think about how you talk to yourself and ask yourself if you would say those words to your kids or your best friend. The answer is always no or never. We don't even realize the impact of our words on ourselves, but we do when it impacts someone else. The more your brain hears something, the more it believes it. Starting today, please stop putting yourself down. We often look at the weaknesses in others in order to make ourselves feel better, but that just reinforces our own insecurities. When we are positive in our thinking, we surround ourselves with positive energy, which brings in creativity, balance, flow, and self-love. It's the nurturer and intuitive inside of you, also known as your feminine spirit.

Every man and woman possess feminine (and masculine) energy. Your feminine energy is expressed in your being when you move with the flow of life, embrace your creative energy, dance, play, and attune to your internal process. Our feminine energy is what desires to feel and experience love. In society, we misinterpret femininity as weak and needy rather than recognizing its power, beauty, and strength. My whole life, I felt like I was playing a gender-specific, feminine role—sit and look pretty, smile, speak when spoken to and be careful not to be too outspoken. If you disagree, keep it to yourself. Go along with what people tell you and don't stand out. I equated femininity with everything it isn't and leaned on my masculinity because that was where I saw strength in myself. In fact, it is where I felt confident. What I learned is that masculine energy is about taking action, being competitive, goal-focused, and being challenged. Those words don't have a lot of love or compassion in them. On the other hand, feminine energy is a deep inner connection with our authentic self, where you seek love from within.

Through my own experience and coaching my clients, I have learned that finding balance after divorce is challenging because we lean into our masculine energy (DOING) and avoid our feminine energy (BEING). If we are busy, organized, and checking off to-do's, we feel like life moves faster. If we are calm, nurturing, and feeling, everything feels slow. So, we choose our masculine energy, thinking it will accelerate our healing, and it prolongs our pain and creates imbalance. Leaning one way vs. the other doesn't work either. I have learned that the goal is to harmonize both energies in our bodies. Don't get me wrong, there will be times when we will lean into one energy over another and vice versa. This is why the concept of balance does not always look the way we think it should. However, we can always strive for harmony in our energetic state. The key here is to connect with your heart and intuition, which connects you with self-love and your feminine energy. It is about honoring your emotions instead of trying to hide or deny them. Our worth is not found in "doing" more. That places our self-worth and value in things outside of ourselves. It keeps us in a state of continuously seeking external validation, even with self-love.

When we identify ourselves with anything other than love, we are living an illusion. My version of self-love was through the expectations of others and not from myself. One of the ways I believed I received love was to obey my elders and family and do as I was taught. My grandparents were Holocaust survivors and came to this country with nothing and didn't know the language. Their goal was to live the American dream and become all things American. The problem with that was it meant don't stand out or call attention to yourself. To be American meant blending in. I was anything but someone to blend in. However, that was what I was forced to do. In other words, I was silenced and unseen. Anytime I spoke up or drew attention to myself, I was shamed. It felt awful and was the last thing I wanted to feel.

I wanted to be someone they loved, were proud of, and felt lucky to call their daughter/granddaughter. That meant closing the door on my true identity and assuming the role I was brought into this world to fill.

My job was to get an education, good grades, marry a doctor or a lawyer, have kids, be successful and become a respectable member of society. It was all about appearances, and I got good at making my appearance seem "perfect." Inside I was anything but that. I was conflicted, unhappy, and confused. I knew that in order to keep up appearances and keep the peace, it meant nodding my head yes and listening to what I was told. It didn't matter if it was what I wanted—it was what made me look good and, in turn, my family. All of who I was, all of what I knew about myself came from the lens of my family and then my husband. I didn't know where I ended, and he began. We were one.

I lost myself and only identified as an "us." I made decisions based on the well-being and likes of that duo. I will never forget the first birthday I celebrated post-separation, and my parents asked me to pick my favorite restaurant so they could take me to dinner. I had no idea where to pick because I would pick a place I knew "we" liked. In fact, the more I gave up on myself, the less familiar I became. Eckhart Tolle said, "When you lose touch with yourself, you lose yourself in the world." When we view our sense of self externally, it means we are no longer coming from within ourselves. After my divorce, I had no idea who I was or what self-love was. To be honest, there wasn't a whole lot I could see to love about myself. So, I decided to look at why I lost my self-love in the first place. Because my identity was referenced externally, I prioritized my relationship above myself, not occasionally, but repeatedly. I saw how I sacrificed myself in small and big ways—from insignificant concessions to giving up a career to cutting off a relative. Over the years, a pattern of compliance developed, and new norms were established. As a result, I built up guilt, anger, and resentment that I kept silent. I blamed myself. My self-esteem, autonomy, and self-respect that I had coming into the relationship whittled away. Eventually, I became a shell of my former self.

Fortunately, we can regain our sense of self-love at any time because it starts from within. Love is present at the center of our being —it is your core. And we live in a world where fear feels like truth and love is a lie. Think about what I just said for one moment, please. Why do you think you expect the worst to happen and talk more about your pain and sorrow than your joy and blessings? It's because of fear. We moved away from the TRUTH of who we are out of fear of what others would think and speak. By doing so, we move away from LOVE. And when you move away from LOVE, how can you NOT feel disconnected, scared, lost, abandoned, alone, etc.? When we replace love with fear, we disconnect ourselves from the world and ourselves. It's why you think something is missing.

The missing piece is LOVE-SELF-LOVE. The feeling of disconnection comes from the lack of awareness of who you truly are and what you are capable of being, doing, and having. No matter how long you have been in this place or if you find yourself going back to that place, you get to make a choice—fear or love. Love is always waiting for you to return to it. It is in the center of your heart and BEING. Repeat after me out loud: I AM LOVE. Say it as many times as you need until you believe it. Notice how hard that was for you. Or was it easy? For most of us, it is really hard. Well, saying the words is easy. Meaning each word is a whole different story.

What would be different in your life if you truly believed the words? So instead of seeing it as, "I've never felt this before," see it as, "This is a new opportunity to feel love." It's about shifting into the energy and warmth of loving-kindness and being kind and loving towards yourself to hear and feel the shift within you. Knowing that you can do this for yourself and having gratitude for and towards yourself. Gratitude is the ultimate form of self-love. When we train our minds to focus on gratitude, we quickly and naturally become more positive, optimistic, and loving because we're turning our energy into blessings rather than lack, hopefulness rather than fear. It is harder to talk down about ourselves when we're filling our minds with what we feel grateful for about ourselves. We become less concerned with our perceived flaws when we're focused on being grateful for our strengths, gifts, and skills. We care a lot less about our supposed inadequacies when we're busy being grateful for all the wonderful things around us, like the air we breathe or coffee.

Why? Because gratitude and negativity cannot occupy your mind at exactly the same time. Gratitude is the expression of appreciation for what one has and receives—independent of monetary worth. For example, you might say out loud to yourself, "I am capable, I am blessed, I am strong, I am smart, I am prosperous, I will have a great day today." When I was in the thick of my divorce pain, those statements felt hard so I would think gratitude was hard. Why? I struggled to find things to be grateful for because I felt like I was losing everything I used to rely on—my husband and my mom. My mom and I were both looking death in the face (the death of my marriage and my mom dying from cancer). We felt like we were falling out of the sky with no parachute. I felt so guilty for how I was feeling when my mom was fighting for her life.

How could I be grateful for anything? Being grateful felt uncomfortable and selfish. At the same time, living in fear was not working. What did I have to lose to try gratitude? That is when I realized that having one more day with my mom was something I was grateful for. And then another, and then another. I shared these thoughts with my mom, and I suddenly noticed a shift in her as well. Her will to live was stronger than ever, and we leaned on one another to get through our own personal hell. Our ability to find gratitude every single day shifted our energy to love, and no matter what life threw at my mom or me, we knew we could find gratitude in the now. Watching my mom fight for her life really brought things into perspective for me. I knew I was greater than all those "things," and I had so much to be grateful for. Gratitude taught me how to make the good in my life visible. When you see the good, you increase your self-esteem, and when you increase your self-esteem, you value and see your worth. Up until this point in my life, I defined my worth by how long my to-do list was, my job, my paycheck, how many friends I had, and what people thought of and said about me, to name a few. And now I was going through a divorce, so you can imagine how the word "divorced" just added to my shame and low self-worth.

When your entire self-worth is based on external things, imagine not only what happens when they are removed from your life but, more so, what you go through to keep them in place. We become people-pleasers and create a life that mirrors what we think we're supposed to have, but it is not in alignment with what we truly desire. Can you relate? I searched for ways to improve my self-worth, and the best way I found was through self-care. When we take care of ourselves, we are showing ourselves that we are worthy of love.

We value ourselves when we practice self-care and we put our needs first! The wonderful thing about self-care is the more we do it, the better we feel about ourselves. For me, self-care is not just the big things, such as going for a massage or spa, but all the little things we do for ourselves, like taking a walk or making a cup of tea. It can be so easy, especially if you have kids, to forget about your own needs and wants. That's why self-care is so important. Doing things that bring you joy will help you feel really good about yourself. You will become a lot happier and able to handle life better. So, make a self-care plan!! Write a list of all the things that you love, bring you joy, or make you feel relaxed. It is how we fill up our own self-worth cup!

Chapter 7

I was really bad at self-care when I was married because I never asked for it nor was it given to me. I felt guilty asking for "me" time and yet my ex-husband had no problem with it. My assumption was if he was so good at it, surely, he will see how much I need it too and he will give it to me. Nope. I relied on him to be my voice and tell me when self-care was possible, and I perpetuated this dynamic in our marriage while blaming him for it. Marriage takes two people, as does divorce. Many times, it is easier to point the finger and blame someone else, especially the one we think is at fault (and that would never be us). In my case, I blamed my husband for my lack of self-care and because he cheated. My kids blamed me. We all need something to blame to justify why it is happening. However, what I learned the hard way (and I am making it easier for you) is you must acknowledge your role and take 100% responsibility for your half and your half only. That means owning who you were, what you did or didn't do, how you showed up, how you acted, how you spoke, or perhaps how you didn't speak. I thought it felt so much easier to blame him, but all it did was keep me in anger, bitterness, and resentment. It kept me pretending about why our marriage fell apart, and it kept me stuck in my past. It's time to cut the bullshit. The sooner you own your side of the street, the faster your healing will take place.

I refused to take responsibility for the first two and a half years. I wanted him to "pay" literally and figuratively, so in my mind, I was punishing him. The problem was, in reality, I wasn't. What I was doing was drinking the poison, expecting him to die, and the only person dying was me. We spend so much of our energy being mad, projecting our disappointment, thinking the other person will feel it and they don't. They live in a world of denial with their own beliefs and thoughts. We cannot influence or change anyone; we can only change ourselves and how we choose to react or respond to them. What I learned was I had to focus on myself and on what I could control and change because I was not in charge of his choice to change or not. It didn't matter how hard I tried or how loud I yelled. I think part of why I fought so hard to make him change was because I could see who he could be if "he just listened to me." After too many failed attempts, I decided to stop and give that energy back to myself. It was depleting me to try to give it to someone who didn't want it or me.

I slowly started to see how my actions toward my ex during our divorce were no different than how I showed up in our marriage. I picked fights to get his attention, communicated loudly, thinking he would hear me for once, and got mad at him for not "getting it" or me. I would make up conversations in my mind thinking he could hear me or read my thoughts. I had this strong belief that because we had been together since we were 18 years old that he should know me, know how I think, know what I want and need, etc. What frustrated me during our entire marriage was quickly realized when we divorced—he is not a mind reader and never knew what I wanted or needed. And I never verbalized it with words that he could hear. I spent so much time being angry with him when it was me who never used my voice to ask for it. #Micdrop moment for me.

I judged myself for wanting to speak up and kept telling myself I would be alone if I did anything different than what other people wanted from me. Here I was in my marriage, trying to "do it differently," and it wasn't working. We weren't getting divorced because of his affair. His affair made it easier, sure. We were getting divorced because we grew apart, and I had a role in pushing him away. I did not like admitting this, and it did not mean it justified his affair. What it did was show me how our marriage declined over the years, and it started with how I showed up as a result of what I learned in my childhood. I knew I had to go inward and work on my inner child, who had so many wounds to heal. In fact, working with my ThetaHealing® mentor helped me to navigate this. There were beliefs I held about being abandoned and alone that were tied to using my voice. Regardless of whether I used my voice or not, I was still not heard and feared being abandoned by those I loved. In my childhood, I felt unseen and unheard. In my marriage, I felt abandoned and invisible. Through digging deep into my past and generational wounds, I was able to see how I had a story around connecting with people and a fear of being abandoned. It was something I desperately wanted to change and heal so that I could feel connected, seen, and heard. To me, that meant love. I worked with my ThetaHealing® mentor to change the belief that to love means abandoning yourself. I wanted to feel love no matter what. I was astounded at how well and quickly it worked because suddenly, I was having co-parenting conversations with my ex-husband and didn't feel the need to raise my voice, nor did I get agitated by his words. I couldn't believe it! It was as though I could see, hear, and speak for the first time in my life. A whole new world opened up to me where I was listening to understand instead of listening to react.

Dr. Stephen R. Covey says, "Seek first to understand, then to be understood." I had it backwards my whole life! Listening to understand is far more powerful than you might realize. Listening is a skill—and one that does NOT come easily when we feel unheard, unseen, wronged, or angry. One of the main reasons why it's so difficult for us to listen and really hear what someone is telling us is because of fear. Whether it's the fear of not being heard, accepted, or respected or the fear of being rejected, misunderstood, judged, or emotionally abandoned, it's always fear that prevents us from consciously listening.

It is difficult for us to listen and really hear what someone is saying because we are afraid of being rejected, abandoned, disrespected, misunderstood, or unseen. So, we listen through the lens of our fears and distance ourselves further from the person and conversation. When we stop listening consciously, we create disconnection from their words and immediately go into "flight or fight" mode. Suddenly we assume there is a problem, and we feel threatened, so we stop listening. When we feel threatened, and a finger is pointed in our faces, we go into fear projections and stop listening. We project our own version of reality onto the other person. We translate their words, body language, and actions through the lens of our fears, beliefs, expectations, and judgments. When this happens, we are no longer in connection with them, and we start feeling the effects of separation, miscommunication, and inner and outer conflict, i.e., more fear and more projections. Sometimes, it is obvious that we have lost rapport with others because we're in full-blown, knock-down fights. Other times, it is more subtle, like when we feel some tension in the air, disconnection, or discomfort. Either way, we cut ourselves off and shut down our listening abilities.

That is the moment we stop listening consciously and are stuck in projection mode. Our fears, beliefs, expectations, and judgments create a wedge between us and whoever we're communicating with. When that happens, we lose the capacity to eliminate the fears, beliefs, expectations, and judgments of whoever we're attempting to communicate with from what they're saying. How can we then truly understand what they are actually trying to communicate if we are projecting our fears? We can't. If that is the case, what results do you think you get from such communication? Fear-based communication only leads to fear-driven results.

When we are in a state of fear, we lead with fear-based thinking. Our mind defaults to how we have always reacted or responded. Listening to reply or react is the standard way most of us communicate, which means that instead of paying attention to what the other person is saying, we are already thinking about what we want to say in response. We tune out the rest of the sentence the moment we react to words being spoken, and it is usually before the sentence is completed. It is great to have a well-thought-out reply, but if you're thinking about what you want to say while the other person is still talking, you aren't really listening and communicating well. You are half listening.

Perhaps you are getting your point across—or perhaps not if the other person listens the same way you do. It is not possible to react and listen at the same time. When we get triggered and start reacting with fear, we go into an endless cycle of projections. And when we project, we are no longer listening, except to our own fears. Fear itself tells us to run, pain in inevitable. When we react to our pain and to the projections that we make of more pain to come in the future, we get entrained in projection mode into the future. If you are caught up in the future, you cannot be listening. You are too busy micromanaging and controlling all the ways in which things could go wrong. If we were able, in that moment of triggering, to stop projecting our fears onto the situation, we would be able to listen once again.

When we listen outside the lens of our fear, we have the capacity to focus completely on what others are saying without reacting to our projections of the implications of their words, body language, and actions. Listening does not mean agreeing with what the other person is saying, nor does it diminish your beliefs by hearing another perspective.

Listening is transformational in that when someone feels listened to, they feel heard, they feel valued, they feel important, and they feel understood. Understanding is powerful and builds respect and trust with another person. When we listen to understand, we gain insight from what they have to say. In turn, it reduces the chance of miscommunication and eliminates conflict, anger, and resentment because we do not assume what someone is thinking and feeling.

I was good at making assumptions about everything and it contributed to the many years I spent feeling angry, resentful, and bitter at my husband. I was unable to acknowledge, approve, or listen to his feelings because I disagreed with them. I immediately turned on the defensiveness switch, overreacted, picked a fight, and raised my voice. I was unable to understand his feelings because I disagreed with them. It was never about needing to feel the same way. It was about respecting that his feelings are different and that it is okay to agree to disagree. I believed there always had to be a winner and a loser. One person was wrong, and the other was right. No exceptions.

I was raised in a home where it was normal for one person to be right and the other wrong. The concept of two people having two different perspectives and both being "right" was not something I understood. It took my divorce to teach me that two people can feel and see things differently, and that is okay. In fact, it is common. When we bring our own experiences and pasts into a relationship, we see through the lens of our experience, which is unique to us. For example, when I was told someone's feelings were hurt, I would immediately tell them they were wrong simply because that was not my intention. I had to learn that even if something was not intended, it still has consequences. Consequences do not mean punishment. It means there will be an action taken. Sometimes action comes in the form of words to communicate how your feelings were hurt as a result of the other person's actions. That is how I quickly learned the saying, "I get to have my feelings, and you don't have to like them." In fact, I taught my kids the same line, and they sometimes say it back to me when we are in a disagreement. It makes me proud every time!

Acknowledging others' feelings and their perspective is not the same as agreeing with or endorsing their perspective, their feelings, or their analysis of the situation. It is also not the same as agreeing to requests they are making. We can acknowledge people's feelings and perspectives without agreeing to any request and without approving or endorsing their underlying feelings. We all desire to feel understood, seen, and recognized and have our own reality validated, but we don't always get what we want. Regardless, it is okay to acknowledge the other person's perspective without meeting all their desires or needs. That is not your responsibility. What is your responsibility is how you show up, how you react, and how you respond. And you must be willing to take responsibility for your actions like I was.

It takes two people to get married, and those same two people play a role in that marriage. Therefore, both parties contribute to the downfall of the marriage. You don't just wake up out of nowhere one day and declare today is Divorce Day. There are always events, actions, and behaviors that lead up to it. In my case, I only saw him and his affair as the reasons for our marriage falling apart. After all, he is the one who cheated. I sacrificed, I put everyone else first, I gave him the space he asked for, and I was a martyr. It wasn't until I saw how I showed up in that martyr role—or rather when the bolt of lightning struck and woke me up—that it occurred to me that I pushed him away with my behavior. Another #micdrop moment for me.

Instead of taking responsibility, I made excuses for my behavior, like the way he stared blankly at me, caused me to yell, or I made him the scapegoat by saying, "he never listened," or "he should have known." I was really good at playing the victim card because it made me feel better for pointing the finger at him. Or at least I thought it did. None of it worked, no matter how hard I tried or how loud I spoke (yelled). I never got the results I wanted. Why? I was mean, and I withdrew because I felt neglected and stopped trying to change things. I justified my actions until I couldn't anymore. While it felt easier to blame him in the short run, it did not pay off in the long run. I see so many women struggling in the same way I did. We refuse to clean up our side of the street and instead create a diversion somewhere else, hoping no one will see it is really us. We think it is easier to blame our spouse than to point the finger and look honestly at ourselves. I was good at sweeping my issues under the rug or blaming someone else because I didn't want to know what it would say about me or my actions. I didn't want to hear that I was not good at that relationship, that I hurt him too, or that I was not as good as a wife/partner/friend as I should have been. Or did I?

Brené Brown says, "When you own this story, you get to write the ending." As women/moms, we think we cannot take responsibility and be free—when that is totally not true! We all get caught up in the routine of life, and yet we don't take control of the vessel that is our life—we wait for someone else to do it or notice that we should start to pay attention. That is why we are so quick to blame outside forces vs. take responsibility. Guess what—you played a role in where you are in your life today, aka you steered your life this way. Owning where you are and your role in getting there is your first step to freedom. It reminds me of my client, Lindsay, who was blindsided by her husband asking for a divorce and lived in the "why" around it. Yet whenever she talked about her marriage, I noticed how bitter she was towards him never being home and never having "me" time, and yet she never had a conversation with him about that. She never asked him to help or be home at a certain time one day per week or on the weekend. Instead, she created a story in her mind around it and treated him with disdain and anger for not reading her mind—sound familiar?

Acknowledging and accepting responsibility for your role in the demise of your marriage is the most vital step in your healing journey. It does not mean you are a horrible person, nor does it mean something is wrong with you. It means that you are human, and you are learning. Sometimes we learn the hard way, and other times it feels easier. I know far too many women who stay stuck in the "I cannot believe he did this to me" page for far too long, and that is not what I want for you! The longer you stay a victim of your circumstances and in negativity, the longer you have low self-worth, lack confidence, and will continue to self-sabotage. It is hard to recognize it for ourselves. I remember the struggle well. In order to move through the healing and recovery process, it takes practice and accountability from someone that is not you.

Have you ever made a list of goals and thought to yourself, "Tomorrow morning, I'm going to wake up and get started!" But tomorrow morning comes, and you think, "I'm going to sleep a bit longer. After all, rest is important, right?" So, you rest and finally start your day. Then, just as you're going to go to the gym, a friend calls and asks to get together, and you think, "Why not? Social interactions and fun are important parts of living a healthy lifestyle, right?" You set out with your friend, and you start giving in to things that you are enjoying but know aren't the "best" choices, as well. Your desire to start fresh "tomorrow" has come and gone, and you wake up the next morning thinking—why can't I just make myself do what I need to do, especially when I want to do better? Because we are really good at making excuses for ourselves.

You are not alone. Accountability from others is a game changer when it comes to accomplishing tasks, sticking to our goals, and breaking free from harmful habits and lifestyle choices. Excuses are suddenly not tolerated. We hold ourselves to a larger accountability scale when others are involved. True accountability is fully owning everything that happens in your life, including your attitude, actions, reactions, teamwork, communication, and relationships. The bottom line is no matter how many motivational posts, self-help books, or informational articles you read, you must still do the work consistently. You have to hold yourself accountable for the choices you make and the consequences they bring consistently. While there are some instances where things are out of your control, learning what is within your control, how you respond to those circumstances, and how you decide to approach all the other situations is entirely up to you.

When you learn how to hold yourself accountable consistently, you are learning how to value yourself as well as the task at hand. Accountability is a game changer because it accelerates your performance and speeds up the process of getting things done. It helps you measure your progress and gives you a better understanding of where you stand and what needs to be done to improve. Accountability keeps you engaged as you see results and helps you focus and stay active in your pursuit of accomplishing whatever tasks are at hand. Accountability keeps you in check and helps you take ownership, so make it a new habit you commit to. When you have a well-developed sense of self-accountability, you are honest with yourself, and you are responsible for what you say and do.

We aren't meant to do things alone. It is important to have people by our side to help us, teach us, support us, keep us in check, challenge us, call us out on things and encourage us in our journeys. But like we said before, unfortunately, sometimes the people we rely on, like friends and family, let us down, or we feel like a burden, so we feel like we have no one to go to. That is why it is so important to have a tribe and leader who has walked the path before you and knows where the landmines are so you don't step on them. They teach you what to look for and how to change direction to ensure success. It is possible to find someone to teach you how to keep yourself accountable as you inch closer and closer to becoming the best version of yourself!

One thing that almost all my clients struggle with is the ability to be both accountable for their words and actions and have compassion for themselves when they fail. You know the cycle...set a goal, try, fail, beat yourself up...set another goal, try, fail, and beat yourself up even harder. Those darn inner critics! What if, instead, we learned how to keep ourselves accountable in a way that is easier? Like treating ourselves as we would a friend in a similar situation. More likely than not, we would be kind, understanding, and encouraging toward ourselves, which is known as self-compassion.

Self-compassion helps to calm our inner critic. It doesn't involve judging yourself or others. Instead, it is noticing that you are suffering and meeting yourself with a voice filled with kindness and warmth amid that pain. It is caring for yourself and your inner critic in moments when you're hurting. Self-compassion shifts you out of danger mode into safety mode. My favorite way to think about self-compassion is, in those moments, to treat yourself like you would your best friend or child. Kristin Neff, a pioneer in the self-compassion field, says, "With self-compassion, we mindfully accept that the moment is painful and embrace ourselves with kindness and care in response, remembering that imperfection is part of the shared human experience." We give ourselves the support and encouragement we need rather than being cold and judgmental. I wouldn't say, "You suck, get over it." I would instead say, "This hurts. What do you need?" and then meet that need. Speaking to yourself like this is the core of what self-compassion is all about.

Most of us are overly critical of ourselves. We have a front-row seat to all of our flaws and weaknesses that are under the spotlight on a stage. It's far easier to be critical of yourself than others, partially because you know your soft spots better than others. It's also easier because being mean to yourself often happens internally, so others don't see it and call you out on it. When you're mean to others, it gets noticed. With self-criticism, you can fly under the radar. Self-compassion is possible to cultivate, even if you dislike yourself. It just takes practice. You don't have to believe it at first. Keep practicing. Right now, you've got a superhighway of self-criticism and an overgrown, neglected path of self-compassion. It takes time and consistency to cut a new path and turn the self-compassion path into the highway default.

Calling yourself bad or shaming yourself for doing something wrong is very different than actually holding yourself accountable. Accountability and shame are very different. Accountability is part of self-compassion, and shame and compassion cannot occupy the same space. Shame does not promote behavior change, compassion does. How? Self-compassion can look different—it can be softness and gentleness, and it can also be calling yourself on your shit! Self-compassion, when tied to accountability, means honoring your values and how you want to show up in the world while not focusing on your mistakes. One of my core values is integrity, and when I did not own my side of the street, I was not in integrity with myself. And it is okay that it took time to see that. Remember that self-compassion is not about letting yourself off the hook. It's about being kind to yourself, and, at times, that kindness means telling yourself that you did something outside of your value system and committing to doing better.

Seeing my role in the downfall of my marriage took time for me to see, and that is okay. There were other steps I had to take to get myself there, and the universe knew that. When we try to skip steps or go out of order because we are impatient or tired of waiting, that is when the path takes a lot longer. The other piece that got in the way for me was my fear of my divorce defining me. If I am being really honest, I was terrified it would become a permanent tattoo across my forehead. Kind of like the boxes you check at the doctor's office. Single vs. divorced—which do I check? Why does it matter, and what's the difference? I was not going to let my divorce or my husband decide who I was going to be moving forward—that was up to me! He gets to live with his choices and actions. That is not my responsibility nor the reflection I was going to see in the mirror anymore.

It is reasonable to expect that we will fall short of our expectations and goals sometimes, and that is okay. It is more than okay. It is great! It allows us to practice what getting up off the ground and dusting ourselves off feels like. Remember learning how to ride a bike? This is no different (minus the decades of life experiences we have). We stand back up and try again instead of staying stuck in a cycle of self-criticism. That cycle creates self-doubt, hopelessness, and stagnancy. Not to mention, I would go out of my way to NOT do things just to avoid failure. Did you know this is a form of self-sabotage? I bet you didn't even realize it. I would go as far as to say it isn't working for you. In fact, it is demotivating you. One teeny tiny mistake, and we throw the possibility out the window. So how do you respond to your mental failures? Self-forgiveness. This is why self-forgiveness is a necessary step to support our well-being as we strive to create our next chapter.

Chapter 8

Forgiveness is hard and sucks, yet it is the fast-track ticket to building the foundation for your new life. It is a muscle that takes time to develop and will involve changing how you respond to failure. The inability to forgive is tied to the guilt you are still holding on to. For some reason, we think our actions, especially divorce-related ones, are somehow reprehensible, and we feel like the worst people in the world for letting everybody down. We believe we have done something wrong (guilt) and feel horrible about ourselves. The guilt is uncomfortable, and it pokes at you. Everywhere you turn, you feel reminders of what you did wrong, and you wind up on an endless cycle of feeling like shit. Right now, you are looking at your marriage with 20/20 hindsight, where you have the luxury of picking apart your past self to pieces, and that is just not fair. Sure, you have made mistakes in the past. Who hasn't? Remember that it takes two to tango in a marriage. You will come to accept that you did everything within your power and skill set at the time to make the marriage work.

Forgiveness is a challenge right now because you are looking at your divorce with a warped vision of what it means and looks like. I define forgiveness as accepting what happened and finding a way to move forward, knowing the past is gone. We all make mistakes, and we have the power to not allow the mistakes to define us. It is what we learn and do thereafter that matters. Acknowledge that you are human, you have made mistakes, and you learned from them. We can't turn back time no matter how many times we relive the past. There is no benefit or good that will come from keeping yourself stuck in self-punishment. In fact, it keeps you disempowered. We can only focus on better tomorrows. Forgiveness is necessary for us to truly move on, learn from our mistakes, and ultimately lead a fulfilling life. What is keeping you stuck at this stage is a lack of understanding of what forgiveness looks like.

Forgiveness is a word that we believe has to do with our ex-spouse. That assumption was the hardest and longest part of my healing process because I thought forgiveness meant forgiving my husband for cheating. You might be thinking the same thing, so you can imagine how resistant I was to the concept. Sure, I read books, listened to podcasts, attended free classes (and paid ones), and tried to find one part of forgiveness that I could wrap my mind around. It was hard because, to me, forgiveness meant excusing his actions and condoning his behavior. Hell to the no! Because my perception of forgiveness was rooted in him, I refused to let myself "go there." Saying the word "forgiveness" agitated me. Anytime I tried to, I got angry, my blood boiled, I cried, and the pain of his betrayal would come flooding back. At the same time, I knew this was an obstacle I had to work through and figure out because what we resist persists. Discomfort always finds us and on the other side of discomfort, there is growth, so I dove headfirst.

In the past, anytime I felt discomfort around a topic or learning a new skill, I knew it was something I had to master. Forgiveness is a muscle we need to exercise daily, just like going to the gym and building muscle. If we are being honest with ourselves, it is very messy and complicated, just like divorce. It is also emotional, confusing, and feels like the last thing you want to give to anyone, especially your ex. You aren't about to let someone off the hook. Therefore, we fight for forgiveness because that is the last thing we want. What if forgiveness means we are weak or letting our guard down to be hurt again? Our divorce has created a tremendous amount of pain, and we are terrified to be hurt again. So, what happens next? We start pointing fingers—at ourselves.

My narrative was that I had to have done something wrong to be in this much pain. So, day after day, I chose to re-live the past in my mind. By doing so, I told myself another version of my life, which my mind and body perceived was the truth. Well, the version I wanted to believe was true. Yet when I say words like "maybe, should have, would have," it is past tense, which creates a false reality that never existed. For example, "I should have tried talking to him more." In that thought, I completely disregarded the fact that I *did* try. We were in couple's therapy, and after some time I remembered it takes two people to make a marriage work. I was no longer willing to accept sole responsibility for both of our actions. Marriage takes two people, and we are each responsible for 100% of our half. And I knew deep in my soul that I did my best. And in coming to that realization, I had unknowingly started what I later learned to be self-forgiveness.

A friend of mine introduced me to someone who was hosting a woman's divorce event, and she thought it would be a great networking opportunity for me. It happened to be local and on a weekend when I did not have my kids. I figured it would be great to potentially make some new friends and connections, which I was seeking! So, I registered and attended the event, which was focused on shifting out of your victim mentality. While I did a lot of this work in my coaching program, I saw the value in her methods as she taught us about the relationship between our thoughts and how we feel. In other words, to see how we have control over our feelings because they stem from our thoughts. I was knee-deep in my thoughts which created feelings and kept me from the holy grail of forgiveness, so at the end of the event, I vulnerably shared that I felt really stuck in judgment. I felt like I was gripping judgment so tightly the thought of loosening my grip felt impossible. In fact, it felt like I would lose control and fall back into old patterns if I let go. She empathized and spoke a phrase that piqued my interest because I had never heard it before—compassionate self-forgiveness.

Compassionate self-forgiveness is a gift we give to ourselves because it uses self-love and compassion to help us break free from the limiting beliefs we create as a result of our own judgments. It recognizes that our experiences are meant to teach us lessons, and sometimes we resist the learning. In doing so, we separate ourselves from feeling freedom and ease and stay in pain due to judgment. Judgment restricts our ability to feel self-love and prevents us from growing. If left unforgiven, a judgment then becomes ingrained as a part of our belief system. When a judgment becomes a belief, it guides our unconscious choices to manifest itself into reality and becomes a pattern that perpetuates itself through behavior. What happens next is that we observe our results and judge and evaluate them in the same way that proves our judgment correct. This is why we establish a self-perpetuating cycle that unconsciously keeps us stuck on the judgment hamster wheel.

Did I just hear you say, "OH WOW!" That is what I said when I heard her explain this. Essentially, any judgment disrupts our own peace. And when we judge, which is a constant in divorce, it is an example of and a way to hold ourselves back from self-love and forgiveness. We are not the arbiter of right vs. wrong. It is up to the universe/G-d/spirit. However, we think it is up to us! We think we have that much power and control. So, what do we do? We self-condemn. In those moments of judgment, that is where self-forgiveness comes in because it balances our inner disturbance through the action of giving love to ourselves. Self-forgiveness helps to release the judgment we place on ourselves and allow the flow of love in.

What have you judged yourself about? What mistake did you make that you formed a judgment around that is stopping you from forgiving yourself? Here are a few I wrote down when I answered these questions. I judged myself as not being enough. I judged myself for being unlovable. I judged my ex as a bad father because he was not the version of a dad I wanted for my children. I judged myself as being too controlling. I judged my ex for being selfish. It felt safe and "right" to make those judgments, and yet all it did was keep me stuck in anger and sorrow. When I chose to shift out of judgement, it helped me to see that I was holding myself to standards that were unattainable. It was time to stop speaking to myself so negatively, especially when it did not help correct the mistake or prevent me from making mistakes in the future. Self-forgiveness eliminates the suffering we inflict upon ourselves unnecessarily, which impacts our behavior, relationships, and life.

If you are like me, when you recognize you've done something wrong or learned a new way to do things, you think about how many times you got it wrong in the past, and BOOM—guilt sets in! When a wave of guilt hits you, it feels like a gray, looming fortress built over your world where you feel trapped. Here is the crazy part, though—all the doors are unlocked, there are no guards, and there's no reason for you to stay there. So why do we stay and not leave? The next time you are feeling guilty and are unsure of how to forgive yourself, ask yourself two questions: Is feeling guilty making me productive, and how will this guilt serve me in the future? If you are coming up with a blank answer or saying, "I have no idea," that is the point. Guilt does not serve you. Forgive yourself and release it. Easier said than done, I know because it is how you have always functioned.

Forgiveness begins with you, hence self-forgiveness. We resist the concept because we don't think we are worthy of it and play the victim of our divorce. When we are in a victim mindset, we stay rooted in guilt. Guilt speaks the language of "maybe, should have, would have," which are common phrases that we speak. However, they are not *action* words. They are *passive* words that your guilt uses to make you create a false past reality that never existed. The next time you find yourself saying those words, nip them in the bud with self-forgiveness and self-compassion. If you find yourself thinking this way, say thank you to the thought, acknowledge it, and say, "You no longer serve me," and let it go.

If that does not work, here is another great exercise you can do that really helped me to reframe what forgiveness looks and sounds like:

Guilt thought: I feel guilty because maybe I should have suggested we go to couples therapy sooner.

The forgiveness mindset: We went to couples therapy when we thought we needed it and did everything in our power at the time to fix it. You were brave to try it and should not feel bad about any of that.

Guilt thought: I feel guilty because maybe I should have brought up the fact that we weren't communicating anymore.

The forgiveness mindset: It takes two people for a marriage to work, and you are not responsible for both of you. You did what you could with the strength you had at the time. Be proud of yourself for that.

Now it's your turn. Write down the specific things that are making you feel guilty, then neutralize them with the compassion you deserve. Do this when you feel the guilt sneaking up on you.

The road to forgiving yourself and overcoming divorce guilt can be a long one but showing yourself much-deserved compassion will ease that journey. Forgiveness means you've stopped wishing life would be different. I believe there are three important pillars of self-forgiveness:

1. Release negative emotions directed toward the self.

    When we do something bad, wrong, or against our values, we may be greeted with painful, negative emotions such as shame, guilt, resentment, or anger. We may also have negative thoughts about ourselves, such as, "It's all my fault," or "I'm a terrible person." Self-forgiveness does not mean we skip the step of feeling bad. It simply means that we work through these feelings of self-resentment and then relieve ourselves of them once they've served their purpose.

2. Cultivate positive emotions and direct them inward.

Self-forgiveness requires fostering kind, generous and positive thoughts and emotions toward the self in the form of self-compassion, love, and respect. The presence of positive emotions can make you feel valued by yourself and others. This, in turn, will generate more positive feelings. Cultivating positive emotions will improve your sense of well-being, happiness, health, and empathy. Celebrate your strengths, practice gratitude, be present in life, and always seek the silver lining.

3. Acknowledge and accept responsibility.

If you were to absolve yourself of negative emotions and shower yourself with positive emotions, it would be "half-ass self-forgiveness." True self-forgiveness involves recognizing the "wrongness" of your actions. Forgiving means you accept and own what happened. You accept and own the behavior and are willing to find a way to move forward, knowing the past is gone and cannot be changed. It also means you are willing to show compassion to yourself even while confronting your actions and showing remorse. The key is to treat yourself with the same kindness that you would show to another person. Try to avoid being self-critical and instead be compassionate while still acknowledging that you made a mistake and want to do better in the future.

Making amends is an important part of forgiveness, even when the person you are forgiving is yourself. Someone unknown once said, "Forgiveness is not about letting someone off the hook for their actions but freeing ourselves of negative energies that bind us to them." Whether or not you receive a direct apology from someone who has harmed you, it's still important to seek forgiveness within yourself. This doesn't mean that you need to keep a relationship or close relationship with the person who's hurt you or even that you accept their behavior. It just means releasing your resentment and anger towards them, which is not good for anyone. No matter what's happening, find the strength to forgive and let go so that you can live your life with love and understanding.

I used to believe that I would never forgive my husband because I thought it would mean forgetting or excusing his behavior. I also believed I would be seen as weak if I had forgiven him. What I learned from compassionate self-forgiveness is that we all did our best with what we received growing up. It doesn't look the same for us all, and it is unfair to punish others based on the toolkit they have in comparison to ours. We all have the right to choose new tools to place in our toolboxes or to stick with the tools we have. I quickly realized that my husband was never going to change or gather the tools to help himself. This realization changed everything for me and our co-parenting relationship. I suddenly released so much anger, resentment, and bitterness toward him because it only hurt me. He wasn't going to change, nor did he see himself the way I saw him. He was still the same person - I was the one who changed. And it was no longer my place to tell him my thoughts or share my wisdom. I wasn't his wife. It was now up to him and time for me to let go and release him from the unrealistic expectations I had set.

Part of my journey to release and forgive meant telling him I forgave him in person, and so I did at our son's high school admissions interview. Yes, you heard me correctly. We were standing outside waiting to walk in the door to check in when the thought came to my mind. I wanted my son to go to this school (as did he), and I wasn't going to allow the energy between my ex-husband and me to get in the way of our son's future. I asked my son to give us a minute, and I walked with my husband into the courtyard. I could see the fear on his face, and I immediately told him I wanted to share something important and positive. I cupped his face in my hands and said, "I forgive you." Tears welled up in my eyes as they did in his, and he said, "Thank you. And why are you doing this right now?" I told him that I accepted responsibility for how I showed up in our marriage and how I treated him, and it was time to release my attachment to anger. The choices he made to address our marital issues were not my burden to bear, only mine were. And I wanted us to be the best co-parents to our sons moving forward. I told him I would always love him (and, of course, made sure to tell him that did not mean I was IN love with him) because he is the father of our boys. I care about him and hope he heals so his mistakes don't follow him. Our son watched our every move and even took a picture to capture history in the making. We embraced and heard our name called, so we walked into the interview, which we nailed, of course. He and I were always strong as a team when we were in alignment. For the first time in many years, I felt like we were on a better path to co-parenting apart than being married and parenting together.

Our children deserve to live in a home filled with love, happiness, calm, laughter, and fun. Sometimes that looks like one home, and in my case, it meant two homes. We never get married thinking of a Plan B (aka divorce), and when it is on the table, we will do anything to avoid Plan B. If only we had a choice or could forewarn our future selves of what was to come! The universe has its own agenda for our life here on earth. No matter how hard we try to control the outcome, predict the future, or eliminate our children's pain, we simply can't. We have no control over forces, we can only control ourselves. While we want to reduce or eliminate the pain our children feel as a result of our divorce, we can't. What we can do is demonstrate to them how to navigate the curve balls life throws at them with grace, compassion, and love.

Life is full of curveballs, isn't it?! Here I was, rebuilding my life and co-parenting relationship with my ex-husband while my mom was confronting the reality of her life coming to an end. As I was learning to smile again and find happiness in what I had, my mom had come to accept the reality of what was ahead of her. She started to appreciate and value the time she had left and the impact she wanted to leave on those who loved her the most. Her shift in attitude impacted those around her, especially me. Like me, she had come to accept that G-d had a higher plan for her, and she knew the time she was given was a gift. Even when my mom went to chemo, she did so with a smile on her face, even when she was in pain and hiding it from us all. She would call me on her way home and tell me how she rested and read and chatted with the nurses to make the time go by faster. Her attitude inspired me and made me think about my actions when confronted with challenges. My mom was being intentional with her time and making the best of her situation. She didn't know how much time she had left, so to spend that time being angry was simply a waste. She would always say, "It could be worse." Little did she know, she was right.

Chapter 9

On September 19th, 2021, my mom's healing journey took an unexpected turn—for the worse. She started a new trial a few weeks prior because her last one was not helping to fight the cancer, and it was too early to tell what impact this new trial would have. Just two weeks before she felt well enough to travel and come visit me and my boys. She was full of energy, feeling good, literally dancing on the dance floor, and upbeat. In just a short time, what had happened between then and now? I was so confused about what I missed or what she didn't tell me.

I was in Mammoth on a getaway by myself (and my dog, Max, of course) and on a hike when it hit me that I had not heard from her in a few days. In fact, she did not return my message on my drive to Mammoth, which is very unlike her unless something was wrong. She usually didn't call when she didn't want me to know something was going on. At that moment, I felt a hard gut punch saying call her now. I increased my walking pace to get to an area where I had better service so I could call her and my dad. Just as I thought my call was going to go voicemail, she picked up, and I could hear in her "hello" that something was wrong. Her voice was raspy and low, not upbeat and energetic like it was just days prior. My stomach tightened because I didn't want to be right again—and I was. I asked what was going on, and she replied that she was back in the hospital because she wasn't feeling well. My mom had issues with her colon as a result of the cancer, and it frequently gave her stomach pain. This time it was too much to handle, so she asked to go to the ER. She had been there a few days and didn't call because she didn't want to ruin my trip or make me worry. So typical of my mom and so upsetting to me. I am not a child and can handle it—although to her, I will always be her baby, and she gets to protect me, even now.

At that moment, I knew in my gut that this was a different trip to the hospital. She had been there so many times before, yet I knew this was going to have a different result. She told me that the cancer was multiplying faster than before even being in this new trial. The doctors were concerned. FUCK CANCER! As she was explaining the doctor's strategy for her care, I could hear in her voice that she, too, knew this was different. I could also hear how exhausted and defeated she was. The kind of tiredness where she was giving up the fight and just wanted to be done. The questions I asked ranged from how are you feeling, to what do they know, to what is your oncologist recommending, to how do we keep fighting, aka how do you keep LIVING? I felt an energy surge to fight for her because I was not ready to say goodbye. It was not her time. I wasn't ready. In my head, I kept telling myself she was going to beat this and be that statistic everyone dreamed of being, not the one everyone else was a part of. I needed my mom, and she was not done on this earth. I wanted and needed more time. I wasn't ready to say goodbye to my rock, my mom, my best friend, and my soul sister.

Like I mentioned before, my mom was diagnosed with ovarian cancer the same day (hours later) that I asked my now ex-husband for a divorce, and we gave one another a reason to get through a shitty time in our lives. I knew she was fighting for me and to show me what strength looked like while I did the same for her. We leaned on one another daily. We cried, laughed, smiled, and strategized together. Her initial diagnosis of Stage 3-C was grim, and we prayed to get at most two more years with her. We pushed for every new trial, every new drug that came out, changed her diet, and I did ThetaHealing® on her. Together, using modern and alternative medicine, we were going to beat this. My mom was open to anything and everything as she knew that her mindset would play such a huge part in her healing. She had been so positive up until that day, and I know that is why we were lucky to get 4 ½ years with her after her diagnosis. She was a miracle, even to her doctors. However, that last visit to the hospital signaled that her cancer had taken the wheel for good.

My mom was ready to go. She even commented to me in her last weeks, "why is this taking so long?" She was checked out and lived waiting to die. It was a version of my mom I never knew, and yet I understood why. My dad was in denial and wanted her to keep fighting. He wanted her to get off the couch and take drives with him, to go out to the park and feed the ducks, and to spend time with him outside of the house. It made him so frustrated and angry. My mom didn't care. She didn't flinch and never wavered. She knew what she wanted, and that was to be in her home, waiting for G-d to take her. It wasn't our choice—it was hers. If she did not want to fight, she did not have to. So, I made my amends with her decision and used the time we had left to ask her questions, pick her brain, and spend as much time with her as possible. Having been through grief before, I knew that was the stage we were headed toward, and I decided to make peace with it instead of fighting it.

What I learned after spending time with my mom in her final weeks and days is that grief takes on many forms. Sometimes it is debilitating, other times, it energizes you and makes you numb. Having been through the grief process with my divorce just a few years prior, I could feel the similarities. It was similar in that I was facing the reality of losing my best friend, my rock, and my mama. The person I called every day to share my life, my daily routine, my work stress, my kids' lives, everything. She always empathized with me and helped me to see what she called "the bright side," which was I had my health. She wasn't wrong in this instance. I wish I could show her that side. I was so focused on healing her that I did not take the time to really be present with her and her thoughts, so that is what my intention was in her final weeks. I wanted her to remember and know the impact she had on my life and my kids' lives.

In her final weeks, I drove up north and visited every other week when I did not have custody of my boys to make sure she knew she was not alone. I also made it a point to kiss her, hug her, sit with her even when she was asleep, send her angel's prayers and tell her she gets to leave on her terms now. I knew this was now in my mom's hands—not G-d's like so many of us say. I believed in my heart that my mom had the power to choose when she was done. Just like I had in my divorce. Separating for one year gave me the time, on my terms, to decide what I wanted and what was best for me— to end on my terms without regret. In the end, it was my decision to end my marriage and begin anew. My mom had the same power. Grief can either swallow us whole, or we can allow it to pass through with permission. With my divorce, it was the former until I made the conscious choice to choose the latter. So, with my mom, I chose the latter because I already had the tools to move through the grief more quickly. I already knew what to do, so I felt prepared and ready to handle the grief this time.

Grief during the holidays that year was especially hard for my dad and me. Every day we wondered if it would be my mom's last. My dad and I rang in the New Year together with the same wish—begging G-d to end my mom's suffering and bring her peace. On January 5, 2022, my mom took her last breath at home with me at her bedside, holding her hand. In those moments before her spirit left her body, I told her it was okay to leave. It was time for her to be at peace, and I would take care of my dad. She could go and find the freedom she so desperately wanted to feel. The night before, my mom spoke her last words to me, which were, "Wendy, you are such a good person, and I love you." I repeated this to myself as tears streamed down my face, and I watched her soul leave her body. She knew she could leave this earth as I was going to be okay and had Jeff in my life. In my heart, I knew she was still with me, and yet in my mind, I was in excruciating pain. It was like I was being stabbed in the heart all over again. No more hugs, kisses, phone calls, text messages, laughter, and mother-daughter shopping. Her physical being left, and while I knew her spirit would always be, I didn't care. I wanted my mom. I wanted her back. I wanted more time.

Time is a funny thing, and I soon realized time is just something we've made up to feel in control and manage our days and nights. The only time that truly matters is the present, and I'm at peace with how I used my last days and hours with my mom. Just the night before she passed, she asked for chocolate and apple juice and said please and thank you. In her sleep, she was waking startled, opening her eyes, and wondering where she was or if it was over. It looked like she was fighting the inevitable and allowing herself to let go. Her body was coming to terms with her next journey and settling into the comfort of knowing her spirit would live on. As I watched her, I felt a wave of peace rush over my body as I heard a message say that my mom would be of greater support and service to me in the spirit realm vs. here on this earth. She knew it was time for her to transition and be my spirit guide and guardian angel. Since that day, I have felt her energy and spirit with me every single day. I can smell her perfume and receive signs that she is with me. She always will be.

My mom had the ability to connect with anyone and everyone. She opened her heart to those who loved her and her loved ones—including my ex-husband. He was her son for 15+ years. He was very close with my mom as my mom always had a special place for him in her heart. When I called my ex to share the news of my mom's passing, he immediately teared up on the phone. I knew how much he cared for her and how embarrassed he was around her because of his affair. Instead of resisting the intimacy of the moment, I leaned into the connection we had around his relationship with my mom by sharing how she felt about him as well as some of our favorite memories of her from our marriage. He reminisced about how much he loved her homemade deli-quality sandwiches she made when we came to visit, the way she swayed when she hugged you, and how she would always say "no offense" and say "sorry" A LOT! My mom's heart was pure gold, and she loved my ex-husband like a son. So, it felt right to share this moment with him. Our surface-level conversation confirmed two things for me— firstly, our marriage was real, which was something I questioned for quite some time, and secondly, I saw just how far apart we had grown. Instead of expressing deep emotions around how he felt, he chose stories and humor. He lacked emotional intelligence and soulful connection, two things important to me in a relationship and exactly what I found with Jeff.

When my mom was diagnosed with ovarian cancer, I thought for sure my ex-husband was going to step up and take me back. I figured the news of her inevitable death was going to wake him up, bring him back to his senses, and he would beg me to take him back. For many months, it did not cross my mind that he wouldn't. What my mind convinced itself of was that he loved my mom so much that he was going to tell me he wanted to try again. There was no way he was going to let me face this alone, and I felt certain he was going to be there for me no matter what. I was half right. He was there for me as a co-parent and helped with the kids when I needed to travel home to help my dad with my mom. As a husband, he was his usual self—non-existent and disconnected. By the time I filed for divorce in December 2017, I knew nothing was going to bring him back, not even my mom's terminal illness. It was a hard truth to face and one that I fought. The harder I tried to get him to see how this was a lesson for him to take me back, the farther away he moved. It taught me that no matter how much I wanted him to see something my way, he never did. It was time to stop wasting energy on him and to focus on me and my mom.

My mother's terminal illness and death taught me that life is NOW. Living is everything, and life is about being present in every moment, every second of the day, and telling those in your life you love them. Stop wasting time with people who don't deserve to be in your life. Give your energy to those that deserve it. Do not allow fear to run your life because, at the end of the day, you don't have control over anything but yourself. What people think doesn't matter. People aren't going to remember how many followers you have on social media or if your kids smiled on your last holiday card. What they are going to remember is the impact you made in their life, the impression you left them with, and the emotion they felt in your presence. My mom left a legacy that I live by every day of my life - health and happiness are all that matter, so do everything possible to live life NOW. You've only got this one - make it your best yet!

Conclusion

I know that was a lot to take in, so let's take a big, deep breath and release it. People make the mistake of thinking divorce recovery work is so hard, but we are the ones that make it so complicated. It's not that it is hard or takes so much time. It takes commitment. What does commitment mean to you? To me, it means making a pledge to something in the future. A promise to do something and be someone. What commitments have you made to yourself lately? I am not talking about commitments you make to others (that is the people pleaser in you). I am asking about the commitments you've made to yourself. I am going to guess you do not keep your commitments to yourself or make excuses as to why you do not have the time to. I sure didn't! You put yourself last on the list, don't you? Be honest with yourself, please. The only one you hurt when you are not being honest with yourself is you. You drink the poison expecting someone else to die. Reality check—you are only killing yourself.

How you treat yourself indicates how high or low your self-worth is. In other words, how much you value yourself and your time. If you are a mom like me, time doesn't always feel like it belongs to us. We feel like our time is shared with others who have needs, wants, and requests of their own. The truth, however, is that we all have the same 24 hours. If someone asks you to do something, they are taking that out of their 24 hours and placing it in yours. Are you the best person to do it, or do you just always default to being the one to do it? Have you built the kind of relationship with that person to justify giving your time away? We need to extend that thinking to our own time, too. "Self-care" has become a buzzword, but it does not just refer to massages or bubble baths—it means dropping out of a committee so you have time to exercise. It can be as simple as ditching your daily Netflix habit and working on your long-awaited side hustle instead. To do any of that, however, you have to learn to value yourself so others will, too.

It starts with learning your values - what makes you who YOU are. Your divorce is not YOU. It is your current marital status. It is a verb, an action. It is not WHO you are. Women who get divorced come from all types of backgrounds – there isn't a one-size-fits-all divorcee prototype. I thought there was at the time, and I definitely didn't fit what I thought was the mold. To me, the mold was a couple that everyone knew was in a miserable marriage. They fought all the time in public, and their kids were disruptive, just to name a few. Here I was, living what I thought was the opposite life when in fact, we were all of those things behind closed doors. Like many, we like to project what I call a "Facebook façade life," where in public, we looked perfect, and behind the scenes, we were living anything but that kind of life. I knew there had to be more women out there like me—hiding from the reality of their situation and pretending it was all going to be okay.

Let's be honest—everything is far from okay when you are pretending. If you want to change your ways, it is time to make a mindset shift because your mindset impacts everything. It impacts your attitude, your confidence, your clarity, your commitment, and your ability to heal. The snowball effect from there is that your mindset impacts every choice and decision you make. Are you willing to shift your mindset from glass half empty to glass half full and create a different life for yourself? In order to shift your mindset, you get to acknowledge and accept the following. Say the following statements out loud after you read each of these because voicing them out loud locks in these realities.

1. Every choice has a consequence. I accept and acknowledge this truth.

2. Change comes from commitment and effort. Yes, I acknowledge and accept this truth.

3. Stumbling, falling down, and making mistakes is a part of the process, not an end to the work. Yes, I acknowledge and accept this truth.

4. I want to be brave. I get to be brave and face my truths, which sometimes means being told things I don't want to hear and being asked tough questions. Yes, I acknowledge and accept this truth.

5. Investing in myself is important. It is worth the time, the money, and the effort. Yes, I acknowledge and accept this truth.

By saying those statements out loud, you stepped over the line and committed to changing your mindset. No going back now! At this moment, that is the biggest game changer that I can teach you because the next step is to create a strategy and plan for your new life, a new road map. Take a moment and ask yourself what gets in the way when you try to create a strategy and plan. Is it procrastination? Is it the temptation of another activity or social media? Is it the fear of making a bad or wrong decision? Is it to numb out? All of these questions have the same answer in common. It is your mindset. As David Cameron Gikandi said in *A Happy Pocket Full of Money*, "Mind your mind." We create what we think, which means we make choices and decisions based on what we "think" will happen instead of what we want to happen. Is what you are afraid of any worse than where you are now, or is there a 50/50 chance that your circumstances could improve if you made a shift? You already know the results of deciding not to deal with your emotions around your divorce. Your results are the same as mine—you stay stuck in your pain.

I know you don't want to be in pain anymore and are tired of feeling stuck when you feel like you are trying to move forward. You're winging it, drowning in quicksand. You're just trying to get through another day. You are doing whatever is necessary to get yourself to bedtime. You live a life on autopilot where accountability does not exist. Your autopilot is called fear. Your fear is keeping you on the same path, and you are living the real-life Groundhog Day movie. You feel like you are being presented with the same situations, and you try different ways to react to them, and you are still not getting the outcome you want because you are afraid that what you want is not possible. Fear is not real—it is <u>F</u>alse <u>E</u>vidence <u>A</u>ppearing <u>R</u>eal.

When you identify your fears, you shine a light of love into those dark corners. Love is light and brings in compassion and curiosity to replace the fear in the dark. The ability to move on after your divorce entails walking out of the dark and into the light, letting go of the past, and leaving behind emotional baggage and negative emotions. My goal with this book is to empower you to start the process of accomplishing this to release the heavy burdens you have been carrying the weight of. Does your back hurt? Would you like to release the weight and feel light again, to allow love and light to flow in and make life easier? I know you desire to feel t peace and freedom.

Without freedom from the past, you will stay stuck on the "ick" of your past, which means no present to experience and no future to look forward to. It is like being in quicksand. The more you fight the inevitable, the further you get stuck and sunk in. Are you stuck and immobilized by the "sand" of your divorce? In order to get out of quicksand, what do you do first? Stop moving and breathe. When you stop fighting, you will stop sinking. Part of moving through the life transition of divorce means letting go of the fear of the unknown and the past. In order to have a beginning, there has to be an ending. And when one door closes, another one opens. You just have to listen and open your eyes.

In order to let go of the past, we must accept our new reality, our life now that we are divorced. It is a part of coming to terms with the loss. To refuse to accept a loss keeps us rooted in fear of the loss. The loss here is our marriage, the life we envisioned, etc. To live in fear is to live under a black cloud that keeps us stuck in the ick, aka the past. Loss is inevitable - like death and taxes! It happens. There is no way around it so let's face it together and come to terms with it! What would life look like with freedom from fear? What is staying in fear costing you? It is the fear that gets in the way of our happiness, peace, freedom, and love. Release fear and give yourself the gift of your life back, on your terms, and created without permission.

One negative feeling, like fear, has the power to create thousands of thoughts that convert into energy and ignites a story in your mind that is rooted in judgment. The voices are your inner critics, and boy, are they loud! We naturally have an easier time believing the negative. Many of us struggle with this, and it is especially difficult during a divorce. Why? Any time you are making a choice in life, usually when it is a new choice, an inner voice alarm goes off that is trying to hold you back and keep you safe. After all, it is their job to keep the status quo. So, it is no wonder when you contemplate moving forward, and it is different than it used to sound or look. It wakes up your inner critics. The bigger the dream, the bigger the inner critics become that you are wrestling with. The Inner Critic is particularly adept at taking a small piece of the truth and fabricating it into a blanket reason for stopping or never starting. When the Inner Critic is present, you are usually building a case or defending a decision. If you notice yourself battling within yourself, check to see if you are actually battling with your own Inner Critic. The loud inner critic voice is easier to subdue when we can tune into it and hear it more easily. Their voice and the information they are telling you are just one viewpoint you adopted based on destructive early life experiences and attitudes directed toward you that you've internalized as your own point of view. After all, there is a difference between always telling yourself that you are not good enough and reminding yourself that you can work to become better.

The truth is you will never be good enough for your inner critic. This does not mean you will never be good enough, though. What does "good enough" mean? What I know to be true is that our best looks different every day, so we are good enough every day. You get to decide what that looks like for you today and the next day, and the day after that. This is one way of questioning those negative thoughts and asking if what they are saying is true. The majority of the time, those voices are not based on facts. They are based on assumptions that are not real. Predictions are not real. They are one perspective of thousands. And from experience, the way we think something is going to go is never the truth in how it really will happen. Listening to your quieter voice of truth is who knows what is best for you. They do not yell as loud as our critics, which can be hard to hear. However, when you just take a breath, you give yourself a moment to recalibrate, that is when you will hear it. It is that voice that knows your values and your boundaries. It is a voice that is full of wisdom, compassion, courage, clarity, and certainty. It is there, and now you get to take one step closer to connecting with it.

This part of the healing process requires a deeper connection to self and why the spiritual healing journey is so important. When we listen to our inner critic, we stay in our minds and disconnect ourselves from the universe. In fact, we separate ourselves from love. And when we disconnect from love, we disconnect from the voice of the universe, spirit, and soul. It is the voice that says you are loved and accepted exactly the way you are! You are NEVER alone. The universe is by your side all the time, understands you, notices you, and cares about you no matter how trivial you think your life might be. You are loved... even the parts you think are the most unlovable. This is part of your healing and recovery that therapy alone cannot support. It requires an element of spirit and trust in the universe to fully come out on the other side whole

Trusting and having faith in a higher power helps us to see that what is happening in our life is happening for us. While we may not be able to understand it at that moment, clarity will come in time and on the universe's timeline. It requires patience, trust, and surrender. If you are an A-type personality type and control freak (now recovering) like me, this is the hardest part of the process. We want instant gratification in feeling better. We see it as going from 0 to 60 in less than 3 seconds. Unfortunately, it does not happen like that. If it did, I would be a millionaire from having bottled that process up and sold it when I began my business in 2018. Your recovery process goes beyond therapy, self-help books, and counseling because you are undergoing a physical and spiritual transformation, or what I call a spiritual metamorphosis. By definition, metamorphosis is the biological process of transformation that creates change from one form to another. Divorce is a catalyst to a transformation that asks you to release parts of yourself and your life that are no longer of service in order to call in that which does. Transformation is not analytical. It is natural and spiritual, and otherworldly. It requires you to listen to what you have not been able to hear before and are suddenly able to now. It takes practice, patience, and accountability to change on the other side of transformation.

The personal transformations we undergo in our lives are a result of our exposure to external and internal conditions and pressures. Divorce is one of those pressures and conditions that give us the opportunity to go from victim to owner, from unworthy to worthy, and from doubtful to confident. When an original rock is subjected to extreme heat and extreme pressure over time, a profound physical and chemical change occurs in the rock, changing its entire chemical makeup (think of a diamond). Some of the most beautiful and valuable rocks in the world are rocks that have been transformed through intense conditions. There are people in this world that have transformed themselves through unexpected intense and extreme conditions, like divorce. Many of us didn't get to decide. It just happened, so we are rolling with the punches. However, you do have control over how you roll with the punches. Do you duck? Do you block? Do you shift to one side? We have many choices in deciding—the process is easier and faster when you are being trained by someone who has been down the path before. Would you walk into a boxing ring without having trained for it or without gloves? Hell no! It takes the right steps and tools to make you the best version of yourself in that ring and to walk out of the ring with the best outcome for you that day, and sometimes that means losing the fight. Losing changes you. You may not be able to see the change at first because you are stuck in your head about the loss. However, just because the change isn't immediately obvious doesn't mean it isn't happening. In fact, all it really means is that you are increasing the heat and the pressure. You are creating the conditions for a metamorphosis, be it personal, business, spiritual, or whatever, so stay disciplined! Whatever happens, do not relent.

My mom was going through her own transformation and metamorphosis at the same time as me. And it wasn't until her death that it made sense to me. My mom lost her fight with cancer on January 5, 2022, and I was so stuck in my head about losing her. I knew life was going to be different from that point forward, and I saw it through the lens of emptiness, abandonment, and loss. What I did not see was her metamorphosis. In other words, cancer was her metamorphosis. It was what took her from human form to spirit form, and as a result, she has been better able to support and serve me from where she is now. Her physical form here on earth served me and everyone on her path in the way her soul intended. Her soul completed its journey. It was time for her to move forward and serve in a higher way— from the other side. I was able to see through the grief to understand this, and I see her every day. She sends me butterflies to reassure and tell me she is with me. Ironic and yet not.

Butterflies are the result of caterpillar metamorphosis. Scientific research shows it can take a caterpillar anywhere from three weeks to three years to complete that transformation, and it is dependent on its environment. What is the environment you have created for your metamorphosis? Is it putting you on the fast track to transformation or the slow path? I was on the slow path, like many of you reading this book. And while it took me years to do this myself, I get to show my clients the path in under one year. Are you in a place where you are ready to heal and move forward on the short end of the spectrum? Or do you prefer to take the longer route? Both routes have the same gift at the end. However, one path does not guarantee you will ever receive the gift. I don't know about you, but I love gifts and encourage you to see how your divorce will be the best one you ever gave yourself, as I did. So let me ask you this final question - which path do you choose?

Afterword

Writing a book has always been on my heart and on my bucket list. When the thought first came to mind, I didn't know what it would be about or when it would come out. I never thought it would be about my divorce and the metamorphosis I went through as a result. I just knew there was more inside of me to speak out loud for others to hear. I was outspoken as a little girl, and even as an adult, I always loved a microphone and a room. The look on people's faces when I spoke lit up my soul. I could see how my energy was contagious. It wasn't about what I said. It was about how I said it. It was about shining my light so others could feel safe to do the same.

I used to be afraid to shine my light because I was told as a young girl that I was too bright. And any light I did shine was shaded, and eventually, after I married, it was taken for someone else's use. My light was depleted, and it felt harder to shine because I forgot where my power source came from. My divorce gave me the wisdom to see that my power resides within me. Seeking it externally was not going to fix my problem. Becoming a people pleaser and trying to see my reflection in others dimmed my light, not help it shine. When we shine our light, the world becomes a brighter place. My divorce was happening for me to shine my light for others to see, follow, and be inspired by. To see the power from within is what makes it eternal.

Writing this book took power and light. A new kind that I was not aware of at the time I started to write. When I began to write this book in September 2021, I had a clear vision of what the book was going to be about and how it would be organized. So, I started to write using my outline and, after a while, realized it felt more and more challenging. It felt rigid and like I was writing a book for someone else. It had to be a book for me, about me, and about my story. It had to have emotions, lessons, and feelings. It also had to include my mom and her parallel cancer journey. So, when my mom took a turn for the worse in October 2021, I thought it was important for me to get this book out before she passed away.

The more I put pressure on myself to get the book done and to have it read a certain way, the less connected to it I felt. In fact, the last time I wrote was the day before my mom took her last breath on this earth. I was sitting in her room, watching her sleep, and I tried to finish my second chapter. It is not the same second chapter you read here because the day after she passed away, I closed the chapter on my book and couldn't bring myself to open the file again. I felt disappointed in myself and ashamed because I felt like I let my mom down by not finishing it before she died. I was also confused about what the book was supposed to be about. I disconnected from my light that day because my mom disconnected her light from me on this earth.

It wasn't until I visited Sedona at the end of October 2022 that I was able to start writing again. I had completed a new outline before I left, and it felt more authentic to what I wanted to say and how I wanted to say it. Being in Sedona allowed me to see what color my light got to be moving forward. Sedona showed me my light never burned out, nor did it disconnect from my mom. In fact, my light was still connected to my mom and my vision for the book. And while I was standing on top of a vortex, I heard the word metamorphosis while watching a butterfly land at my feet. At that moment, I knew what my book was about. I knew what my light looked like, felt like, and sounded like. It all clicked. My light was dimmed while in my own chrysalis—it was being protected, stored, and transformed. When I emerged from the cocoon, my light shone brightly in my new form as a butterfly. My mom told me through a medium that she would come to me as a butterfly. That was her way of telling me she was with me. On that mountaintop, I felt her, my light, and the power our story was going to have in this world. It was an energy surge that came in through my heart, out through my fingers, and onto the pages of this book.

I could feel the power within me for the first time in decades, maybe even my whole life. I could feel the gift I was meant to give the world and to do so through my words, my story, and my life. This was not a time for me to be shy and keep my experiences to myself. It was time to soar and spread my wings. To use my voice to help others see the lessons that are on the other side of pain. To be the example of what is possible when you choose to do the inner work and commit to change. My journey was not easy, nor did I expect it to be. However, I knew it was one I had to get through in my own time and way. My mom saw that too. I know she would have moved mountains to take my pain away. In the end, she trusted I would get through it. All she had to do was be there for me, with me, and it didn't mean just physically. My mom knew it was time for her to leave this earth so she could be there in spirit to support me as I flew. Being here on earth was not serving her or me anymore. In fact, she picked me to be with her as she drew her last breath. That is the other message I heard on top of that mountain. She chose me. She chose me because she knew I would help her as she transitioned and found her inner peace.

The grief we experience from life transitions like divorce and death is incredibly powerful. We can choose to stay in the sadness of our grief or see our grief as a catalyst to change, to live in the now and see the silver linings. After my divorce, I never wanted to get married again. I was so hurt, so broken that I swore it was never, and I mean never going to happen again. When I met Jeff on October 8, 2020, he changed my perspective on marriage, life partnership, and commitment. So much so that at sunset on August 11, 2022, on the beach in Maui with our boys present, we exchanged vows and rings, committing to what we call a 10 out of 10 life together. That means that we get to have a 10 out of 10 in our life, and when we see that we are not at a 10, we get to work together to get back to a 10. In fact, this is how I live my life. To strive to be at a 10, and when something is in the gap, I look at what gets to shift to get myself back on the path to a 10.

You get to have a 10 out of 10 life, whatever that looks like for you. It can be hard to see what that looks like and know the first steps to take to get there. I get it, and I was there. And after taking the long and winding road, I have created a shorter and straight route for you to take. Receive the gift in my lessons and mistakes to accelerate your healing journey and become the beautiful butterfly I see in you.

Connect With Me:

Visit www.divorcesucksnowwhat.com to download free resources to help you with what I've discussed in this book.

Schedule a complimentary Healing & Support Call: www.contactwendy.com

Join my Facebook Group: The Divorce Rehab®
www.facebook.com/groups/divorcerehabwithwendy

Listen to my podcast, *The Divorced Woman's Guide*, available on all podcast streaming platforms.

The "B" Word course and other courses can be found at www.divorcesucksnowwhat.com under "Courses."

Connect with me on Instagram @divorcerehabwithwendy

Want to know your divorce superpower? Visit my website www.wendysterling.net and take the quiz!

Acknowledgments

First and foremost, I want to thank my dad for giving me the nudge to finish my book. My dad sparked the light inside of me and reminded me of the importance of telling my story. I also want to thank my incredible sons, Adam and Sam, who are my world and my biggest fans! Your unconditional love and support of me during my time away from you to write means everything to me! I also want to give thanks to my partner in love and life, Jeff. Thank you for supporting me in making my dreams come true and being along for the ride. I love you so much!

I also want to give a shout-out to my amazing friends and HCL family for your support, encouragement, and faith in getting this book into the world! It is my book of love! Finally, I want to thank my mentors who supported and guided me along my path to be who I am today—Marlo, Jenn, Kelly, Sara, Shameca, and Corrina.

This book would have never existed if it weren't for my discovery of the magic of Sedona as well as my divorce—or what I call the gift that keeps on giving! So, thank you, divorce—and all the silver linings you shine upon me and my path!

Made in the USA
Columbia, SC
15 July 2024

38657212R00085